BRUCE ELDER

*** Highly recommended
** Recommended
* See if you can

Second Edition 1997
First published in 1995
by New Holland Publishers Pty Ltd
London • Cape Town • Sydney • Singapore

24 Nutford Place
London W1H 6DQ
United Kingdom

80 McKenzie Street
Cape Town 8001
South Africa

3/2 Aquatic Drive
Frenchs Forest, NSW 2086
Australia

ISBN 1 85368 697 2

Publishing Manager: Averill Chase
Managing Editor: Mariëlle Renssen
Editors: Madeleine Jennings, Anouska Good
Design and DTP: Sonya Cupido
Cartographer: William Smuts

Reproduction by cmyk pre-press
Printed and Bound in Hong Kong by Sing Cheong Printing Co. Ltd

Photographic Credits:
Shaen Adey (NHIL), cover (top left & bottom left), half title, pages 38, 41, 54, 57, 112, 117; **Murray Child**, page 49 (bottom); **Bruce Elder**, pages 25, 40, 43, 49 (top), 56, 67, 88, 89 (top), 104, 105, 110, 115, 119; **Anthony Johnson (NHIL)**, cover (top right); **NHIL**, cover (bottom right); **Nick Rains**, pages 4, 6, 8, 10, 11, 12, 13, 15, 17, 18, 19, 20, 22, 24, 27, 28, 30, 33, 34, 36, 42, 46, 52, 55 (top and bottom), 89 (bottom), 108, 111, 114, 118, 119 (bottom); **Ken Stepnell**, pages 7, 9, 50, 60, 62, 64, 66, 68, 72, 75 (top and bottom), 79, 80, 85, 86, 90, 91, 93, 97, 99, 101, 102 (top and bottom), 103.

NHIL = New Holland Image Library

10 9 8 7 6

Cover photographs:
Top left: *An aerial view of Uluru (formerly known as Ayers Rock) captures its vast magnitude and splendour.*
Top right: *The Sydney Opera House is Sydney's premier landmark and an internationally recognised architectural feat.*
Bottom left: *Snorkelling in its underwater coral gardens is one of the Great Barrier Reef's chief attractions.*
Bottom right: *Native to Australia, these cuddly koalas warm the hearts of both young and old.*
Title page: *The Pinnacles in Nambung National Park, Western Australia, feature limestone-encrusted pillars of differing shapes.*

CONTENTS

NEXT 96 km

1
Introducing Australia

Australia is a country of remarkable diversity. It ranges across more than 30° of latitude from the tropics of north **Queensland**, the **Northern Territory** and northern **Western Australia** through to the temperate rainforests of southern **Tasmania**. The great appeal of Australia, with the exception of cool, moist Tasmania which defies every generalisation about the country, is the vastness of the landscape, the extent of the desert areas (it has the second-largest dry desert area in the world after the Sahara), the incredibly blue skies and its richly multicultural society.

Australia enjoys long periods of **sunny, dry weather** and consequently is essentially an outdoor society characterised by informality, egalitarianism, friendliness and a genuine dislike of protocol and pretentiousness.

The strengths of modern Australia lie in the acceptance that this is a country where life is easy, where the narrow social stratification that is so much a part of European society has been abandoned.

Look at Australia on the weekend and you will find sport ovals full and beaches crowded. Watch the main arteries out of any major city on a Friday afternoon and you will find them choked with cars full of bushwalkers, people travelling to their holiday homes, surfers, fishermen and people fleeing the cities. However, it should always be remembered that, although Australians still love the idea of the rural 'bronzed Aussie', less than 15% of the population actually live in rural areas, or 'the bush' as it is called.

Top Attractions

*** **Great Barrier Reef:** one of the wonders of the world with magnificent coral formations and exotic marine life.
*** **Uluru and Katatjuta:** spectacular rock remnants surrounded by desert. Best seen at dawn and dusk.
*** **Sydney:** the beautiful harbour setting, the Bridge and the world-famous Opera House are some of the city's premier attractions.
*** **Great Ocean Road:** dramatic and impressive coastal scenery against a backdrop of rural peacefulness.

Opposite: *Signs warn travellers to watch out for camels, wombats and kangaroos as they travel through the Australian 'outback'.*

Facts and Figures

- **World's largest electorate:** Kalgoorlie, Western Australia, covers over 2,000,000km^2 (770,000 sq miles).
- **Largest property:** Strangeray Springs, South Australia, is the largest cattle station covering 30,000km^2 (115,800 sq miles). It is three-quarters the size of Switzerland.
- **Largest basin:** the Great Artesian Basin covering 1,700,000km^2 (650,000 sq miles).
- **Tallest building:** Centrepoint's Sydney Tower is 324.8m (1065ft) above sea level.

Far removed from the pains and sufferings of the rest of the world, Australia is fast becoming the **working-class paradise** that the people of Europe have dreamt about for centuries.

Visitors to Australia will be confronted by a continent of bewildering diversity. They can experience the tropical magic of the **Great Barrier Reef** with its fantastic coral formations and the vastness of the **Great Artesian Basin** which runs down the centre of the country – an area where steaming bores bring water to the parched land from hundreds of metres below the earth's surface.

They can marvel at the beauty and elegance of the modern cities and wonder at how they can travel for hundreds of kilometres without ever seeing another human being.

In Tasmania they can be seduced by wild beaches where waves, uninterrupted by land since they left South America, crash onto lonely shores, and they can marvel at the dramatic glaciation of the island's cold and forbidding **Cradle Mountain** area, which stands in sharp contrast to the red deserts of the mainland.

Beyond these features there is the gently undulating cattle country between the Great Dividing Range and the Pacific Ocean, the beauty of the **Snowy Mountains** in winter, the vast plains where sheep and wheat sustain small rural communities, the dramatic red soils and beaches of the Kimberley and the huge jarrah and karri trees on the south-western tip of Western Australia.

But no journey around Australia, and no one wanting to understand this mysterious continent, should miss the **'dead heart'**. **Alice Springs** with its dry Todd River and the MacDonnell Range stretching to the east and west of the town; **Uluru**, 'the greatest stone on Earth', always marvellous at dusk and dawn; the huge marbles that are Katatjuta; and the jagged canyons – **Standley Chasm**, **Simpson's Gap**, **Kings Canyon** – are all places seemingly designed by nature simply for the purpose of taking the visitor's breath away.

Opposite: *The Australian passion for the beach, sport and surfing is perfectly expressed in the volunteer surf life-savers who, each weekend, test their skills against the ocean breakers and protect the people who come to surf and relax.*
Left: *Towering above Dove Lake are the jagged, snow-capped peaks of Cradle Mountain. Cradle Mountain–Lake St Clair National Park is one of Tasmania's premier tourist destinations.*

THE LAND

The Oldest Continent

Many regard Australia as the oldest continent on earth. Certainly it seems to be both the most stable and the most eroded of the continents. Geologists have dated parts of the Western Australian shield at 3000 million years old.

Hundreds of millions of years ago, there was a mountain range in central Australia which was higher than Mount Everest. When travellers arrive at **Ellery Creek Big Hole**, one of the many gorges and chasms which split the MacDonnell Range, they will see a notice board near the car park which explains that 'All around you there is evidence of a great mountain-building episode in the formation of Central Australia. You can see tortured folds of rock which formed deep in the earth and when great heat and pressure pushed up 10,000m (33,000ft) of mountains . . . 350 million years of erosion have almost worn them away, exposing the deeper folded rocks'. It is at moments like this that the traveller realises how ancient the continent really is.

The Flat Continent

Australia is the lowest and flattest continent on earth. Only six per cent has an elevation above 700m (2300ft) and the country's highest mountain, Mount Kosciuszko, is only 2229m (7300ft) above sea level. It is scarcely more than a substantial hill and can be reached in an easy day's hike. The continent's largest flat surface is the Nullarbor Plain which covers over 250,000km^2 (100,000 sq miles).

Above: *Lying to the north of Uluru (Ayers Rock) are 36 smaller monoliths known as Katatjuta (the Olgas). It is thought that Katatjuta may have once been many times the size of Uluru.*

To understand the physical shape of Australia it is best to think in terms of **four distinct regions**. Along the east coast (where most of the country's population lives) there is an upland region known as the **Great Dividing Range**. This is a series of plateaux, high plains and spectacular gorges, which run from **Cape York** in northern Queensland to the southern tip of **Tasmania**. Between here and the Pacific Ocean is the most productive land, enjoying good rainfall and moderate temperatures.

Beyond the Great Dividing Range are the **Murray, Eyre** and **Carpentaria basins,** which stretch from the **Gulf of Carpentaria** in northern Queensland through western **New South Wales** into western **Victoria** and parts of **South Australia**. This is the region that early European explorers thought was a huge inland sea because the major river systems, instead of running to the east, run in a southwesterly direction, either reaching Lake Eyre or joining the Murray–Darling basin and flowing into the Southern Ocean at Lake Alexandrina.

Over half of Australia is taken up by the vast **Western Craton**, a series of low-lying plateaux and desert regions which extend from the Barkly Tableland of the Northern Territory across to the Kimberley and Pilbara through the vast desert regions of the **Great Victoria Desert, Gibson Desert** and **Great Sandy Desert**. This is a region characterised by seemingly endless ridges of sand dunes (from the air much of the area looks like an uninhabited piece of corrugated iron) and almost blood-red soil which is rich in iron-ore. This is where nature, over millions of years, has eroded all the major formations – with the notable exceptions of **Uluru**, the **MacDonnell Range** and the strange formations of the **Kimberley** region in Western Australia.

Seas and Shores

Australia is justifiably famous for its coastline. Although it is a country which is almost exactly the same size as USA (excluding Alaska), most of the population live at or near the coast. More than half the towns in the country are located in New South Wales and Victoria and over 80% of the population live in the narrow coastal strip from Cairns in north Queensland through to Adelaide.

There is considerable diversity in this coastline but there is little doubt that the most impressive feature is the **Great Barrier Reef**. It can be seen from the moon and, as every *Trivial Pursuit* buff knows, it is the largest structure on earth built by living creatures.

The opportunity to explore the Reef by pleasure craft, snorkelling or diving is an opportunity to explore a wonderland of exotic fish and magical coral formations.

From Bundaberg through to the north of Victoria the coast is characterised by excellent swimming and surfing beaches (some have international reputations for the quality of their waves) set between low-lying headlands which are popular haunts for fishermen. These conditions continue into South Australia and around much of the coast of Tasmania. At particular points, notably along the **Great Ocean Road** in Victoria and along the west coast of Tasmania, the beaches give way to rugged cliffs and spectacular scenery.

Most of the coast has good facilities for mooring fishing boats and pleasure craft and, where necessary, the local communities have constructed breakwaters and wharves.

Beyond Eyre Peninsula in South Australia lie the dramatic cliffs which fall sheer to the sea at the edge of the **Nullarbor Plain**. It is not until Western Australia that the cliffs again give way to beaches and harbours. One of the country's best kept secrets is the coastline from Esperance to Albany and around to Busselton and Perth. Characterised by breathtakingly white sands and stunning granite headlands, this coastline is arguably the most beautiful in the whole country. Only isolation and the cold winds from the Southern Ocean have protected it from development.

Above: *The north-eastern coast of Victoria is famous for the vast Ninety Mile Beach. A popular spot for quiet holidays, the long beach offers surf fishers excellent opportunities to catch an evening meal.*

Great Barrier Reef

The Great Barrier Reef is Australia's most awe-inspiring natural wonder. Its coral formations, the diversity of the tropical fish which live in the area, and the fact that it is largely untouched by the modern world make it a natural magnet for visitors. The Reef extends south from the coast of Papua New Guinea for over 2000km (1242 miles) to Lady Elliot Island near Bundaberg, Queensland. Divided by scientists into northern, central and southern regions it is in fact an interconnecting series of some 2000 individual reefs and 71 coral islands, featuring over 400 varieties of coral and 1500 types of fish.

SHARKS IN AUSTRALIA

Many overseas visitors see Australia as a country noted for its dangerous snakes, spiders and sharks.

It is true that sharks are widely feared in Australia. Most beaches have shark lookout points and shark patrols. However, while there have been more recorded cases of death from shark attack in Australian waters than anywhere else in the world, it is still true that in 200 years of European settlement there have been fewer than 100 recorded deaths. In fact, sea wasps (the deadly box jellyfish found off the coast of Queensland) have been responsible for more deaths.

The coastline of Western Australia has many beautiful beaches and is noted for its excellent fishing. Of particular note is **Shark Bay** with its famous friendly dolphins at Monkey Mia and the glorious beaches around Broome.

Beyond Broome, around the northern coastline to Cairns and the Barrier Reef, the waters are characterised by mangrove swamps, broad estuaries from the rivers which are swollen by the rains from 'the wet' which sweeps across the coast every summer, and the ever-present dangers of crocodiles, sharks, deadly jellyfish and stingrays.

Climate

Australia is a dry continent. Over two-thirds of the country experiences rainfall of less than 500mm (20in) per annum and more than one-third of the continent (mainly from the centre across into Western Australia) has an annual rainfall of less than 250mm (10in).

However, it is important to recognise that Australia is not just one vast desert. The areas of greatest population – along the eastern coastline and in the south-western corner of Western Australia – typically receive rainfall over 1000mm (40in), substantial snowfalls occur during winter (June to August) in Tasmania and on the Snowy

Right: *The MacDonnell Range, which stretches to the east and west of Alice Springs, is cut by a number of gorges offering a cool respite from the desert heat. Glen Helen, lying 133km (83 miles) west of 'the Alice', is noted for its exceptional tranquillity and beauty.*

Above: *The tiny mining town of Marble Bar in Western Australia is known as 'the hottest town in Australia'. During all the time that records have been kept the temperature at the town has never dropped below 0°C (32°F).*

Mountains (which stretch from southern New South Wales into northern Victoria), and the northern coastline experiences tropical conditions including monsoonal rainfall above 1500mm (60in) and long periods of humid summer weather. Australia lies between the latitudes of 10°41'S and 43°39'S and consequently any generalisations about the climate are very difficult.

It is worth remembering the extremes of the country's temperatures. There was a summer (1923) when the town of Marble Bar in Western Australia recorded temperatures which never dropped below 37.8°C (100°F) for 161 consecutive days.

The period before 'the wet' (December to March) in places like Katherine and Darwin rivals anywhere in the world's tropical zones for heat and humidity and, when the weather is right, the Snowy Mountains have more substantial snowfields than Switzerland.

Right: *A sudden storm will turn Australia's vast deserts into oceans of coloured flowers, but nothing quite compares to the red and black flowers of Sturt's desert pea.*
Opposite top: *Kangaroos rest during the day, but at dawn and dusk it is quite common to see them in outback Australia.*
Opposite bottom: *The Australian deserts are full of extraordinary animals. The thorny devil lives on small black ants and has been known to eat over 1000 ants in a single sitting.*

Looking at Animals

Australia has some extraordinary animals. They can be seen in Queensland at the **Lone Pine Koala Sanctuary**, Brisbane; **Currumbin Sanctuary**, the Gold Coast; and **Green Island Underwater Observatory** off the coast of Cairns. In NSW they can be seen at the **Taronga Park Zoo**, Sydney; **Western Plains Zoo**, Dubbo; and **Ku-ring-gai Chase** and **Wollemi national parks**.

Plant Life

The enduring image of Australia is the eucalypt or 'gum tree' which is found wherever there is adequate rainfall and the land has not been cleared. In its most beautiful manifestation, particularly in the Blue Mountains to the west of Sydney, the eucalypt forest gives the appearance of being lightly brushed with a smoky blue.

It has been estimated that Australia has some 20,000 species of flora which range from the tropical rainforests through mangroves, sclerophyll forests, savannas, mallee scrub and desert. The desert, particularly after rain, is spectacular with the sharp red and black of Sturt's desert pea, which is typical of this harsh beauty.

The best way to appreciate the richness and diversity of Australia's flora is to visit Western Australia when the bush is in bloom. To the north and east of Perth there are literally hundreds of kilometres of bush which come alive with native plants.

Animals

Isolated from South-East Asia, Australia has developed its own, unique fauna. Animals such as the platypus and echidna (both egg-laying mammals) and the marsupials – kangaroos, wallabies, wombats, koalas, numbats and phalangers – have given Australia a reputation as a

country with strange and exotic animals. Indeed, when a dead specimen of platypus was sent to England by early settlers it was thought to be a hoax – a duck's bill attached to an unknown mammal.

Travelling through western New South Wales and western Queensland it is common to be confronted, particularly at dusk, by kangaroos leaping across the road.

There seems to be a popular perception that Australia is a country full of dangerous creatures – deadly redback and funnel-web spiders, large numbers of poisonous snakes, seas full of sharks, stonefish, sea snakes and deadly jellyfish, and rivers with crocodiles waiting for the unsuspecting swimmer. While this is not entirely accurate, it does pay to be careful.

In fact, Australia, with the exception of the dingo, has no large land-based carnivores. Consequently, a large number of land-based animals, with no mechanisms to protect themselves against predators, have developed on the continent. As a result, many native birds and small mammals have been devastated by introduced species – notably feral varieties of domestic dogs and cats. Similarly, the consumption of grass by grazing animals and introduced rabbits has placed enormous pressures on the kangaroo and wallaby populations.

Looking at Animals

In Victoria there is the **Royal Melbourne Zoo** and in Tasmania there are animal sanctuaries at **Mt Field National Park**, **Bruny Island** and **Flinders Island**.

In South Australia **Adelaide Zoo**, the **Warrawong Sanctuary**, Mylor; the **Cleland Conservation Park**, Mt Lofty; **Gorge Wildlife Park**, Gudlee Creek; and **Kangaroo Island** are all worth visiting.

In Western Australia the **Perth Zoo**, **Caversham Wildlife Park**, Perth; **Underwater World**, Perth; **Rottnest Island**; **Penguin Island**; and **Monkey Mia** are famous, and in the Northern Territory there are **Berry Springs** and **Kakadu National Park**.

HISTORY IN BRIEF

The human history of Australia probably started around 55,000 years ago. There is considerable evidence that, at this time, the sea level was 120m (395 ft) lower than it is today, making the journey of the ancestors of Australia's Aboriginal people down through the Indonesian archipelago relatively easy.

Although archaeologists are constantly revising the date of the first settlement of the continent there is definite evidence that Aborigines were established as far south as the Perth area around 38,000 years ago. The important archaeological site at Lake Mungo in far western New South Wales has provided evidence that from 32,000 years ago Aborigines were living in that area and were using stone tools, engaging in ritual cremation, using ochre and eating the crustaceans which lived in the rivers and lakes in the area.

By 25,000 years ago Aborigines had moved into Tasmania. Throughout the country they were painting, hunting marsupials, grinding seeds and mining flint. This culture continued until Europeans arrived and settled at Port Jackson in 1788.

ABORIGINAL MUSIC

The **didgeridoo** is an Aboriginal wind instrument which produces a deep, rich, resonant sound. It is a wooden pipe about 2m (6ft) long and 5cm (2in) in diameter. Complex rhythmic patterns are played using breathing techniques which allow for continuous sound.

Didgeridoos are traditionally used in tribal ceremonies called **corroborees** in which spiritual, festive or war-like intentions are expressed through rituals of music and dance.

The Early Explorers

It is difficult to determine when the first non-Aborigines made contact with the continent. There is some evidence that the Chinese knew of the existence of a southern continent as early as the 13th century and it seems that the great Chinese explorer **Cheng Ho** reached the shores near modern-day Darwin sometime in the early 15th century.

It wasn't until the 16th century that Europeans began to acknowledge the existence of a southern continent. In 1531, a French cartographer put the name Terra Australis on a world map and by 1597, European maps were showing Australia as being separate from Papua New Guinea.

In 1606, the Dutch explorer **Willem Jansz** explored the western coast of Cape York and the Portuguese **Luis Vaez de Torres** sailed between Australia and Papua New Guinea. A decade later, **Dirck Hartog** sighted the northwest coast of Australia and left a pewter plate on an island near Shark Bay in Western Australia.

For the next 150 years explorers continued to investigate the coast. The most significant were **Abel Tasman** who reached Tasmania (which he called Van Diemen's Land) in November 1642, and **William Dampier** who explored the coast of Western Australia in 1699.

Opposite: *Purnululu (Bungle Bungles) are one of the wonders of outback Western Australia. Formed over 350 million years ago, they have the appearance of gigantic bell-shaped rock towers with horizontal banding produced by layers of black lichens and orange silica.*

However, all these explorations and discoveries became insignificant when **Captain James Cook**, having observed the transit of Venus in Tahiti, sailed the barque HM *Endeavour* west and reached Point Hicks on 20 April 1770. Cook sailed along the east coast of Australia and it was on his recommendation that **Captain Arthur Phillip** sailed the brig HMS *Supply* into Botany Bay (now part of metropolitan Sydney), arriving on 18 January 1788. A week later he moved north to the magnificent natural mooring at Port Jackson where he established a convict colony. This was the beginning of European settlement in Australia.

Convicts and Explorers

Australia's European origins were founded in unfortunate circumstances. Following the loss of their American colonies in 1783, the British had decided to establish a penal colony at **Botany Bay**. On board the First Fleet were some 730 convicts (about 570 men and 160 women), 250 free citizens (including many hard-drinking soldiers) and enough plants and livestock to establish a colony.

The Early Struggle

The 11 ships of the First Fleet sailed into Botany Bay on 18 January 1788. Captain Phillip was disappointed with the land and sent scouts north to Port Jackson.
The settlement struggled in the early years. Convicts who had often received lengthy sentences for petty theft were not enthusiastic workers. The arrival of the second fleet in 1790 eased the struggle but starvation threatened the colony. It was not until 1808 that the first shipment of wool was sent to England.

HISTORICAL CALENDAR

c.40 000 BC Australian Aborigines settle continent.
1606 Willem Jansz becomes first European to set foot on Australia.
1770 Captain Cook charts the east coast.
1788 Penal colony established around present-day Sydney.
1808 The Rum Rebellion (Governor Bligh deposed).
1813 Blue Mountains crossed.
1835 Melbourne founded.
1840 Convict transportation to NSW abolished.
1851 Gold rush begins.
1854 The Eureka Stockade.
1876 The last full-blooded Tasmanian Aborigine dies.
1880 Bushranger Ned Kelly captured and executed.
1901 Federation of the states and national independence.
1902 Women get federal vote.
1908 Canberra chosen as site for national capital.
1915 Gallipoli becomes site of tragic World War I campaign.
1942 Darwin and Sydney attacked by Japanese.
1947 International immigration drive begins.
1960 Aborigines granted citizenship (and the vote in 1962).
1961 Massive iron-ore deposits found in Western Australia.
1972 Troops withdrawn from Vietnam after large-scale demonstrations.
1972 White Australia Policy formally ended.
1974 Cyclone Tracy hits Darwin.
1975 Prime Minister Whitlam sacked by Governor General.
1980 Azaria Chamberlain's disappearance leads to imprisonment of her mother – charges eventually quashed.
1993 Mabo ruling opens door to Aboriginal land claims.
1993 Sydney wins bid to host 2000 Olympics.
1996 Lone gunman kills 35 at Port Arthur, Tasmania.

Australia's history from 1788 until 1851 is the story of penal colonies and the development of a European society based on cheap labour and land conquests.

From the moment the convict settlement was established in Sydney there was a rapid desire to explore and exploit the land. Within months of settlement, explorers had covered the entire Sydney basin and were seeking ways to cross the **Blue Mountains** to the west and find new pastures for sheep and cattle. Finally, in 1813, **Blaxland**, **Wentworth** and **Lawson** succeeded in crossing the Blue Mountains and in the period up to 1840 explorers travelled west from Sydney across to South Australia (**Sturt**), south across the Snowy Mountains to the modern-day site of Melbourne (**Hume and Hovell**), north to modern-day Queensland (**Cunningham**) and west to the edges of the desert (**Sturt and Mitchell**).

By 1830, there were some 58,000 convicts in Australia. Many of them, after serving out the time of their sentences, stayed on and acquired land. It was not an easy society. The settlers moved out from the coastal settlements and grabbed any good land they could find. They treated the indigenous Aborigines like animals, thinking nothing of shooting and poisoning if the local population resisted the inexorable advance of western 'civilisation'.

DISCOVERIES AND SETTLEMENT

European Discoveries
1642 - Van Dieman's Land (Tasmania)
1770 - Botany Bay
1774 - Norfolk Island
1788 - Lord Howe Island
1802 - Spencer Gulf and St Vincent Gulf
1819 - Port Essington
1828 - Fremantle
1839 - Port Darwin

European Settlement Dates
1788 - Port Jackson (Sydney)
1804 - Newcastle and Hobart
1825 - Brisbane
1829 - Swan River (Perth)
1835 - Melbourne

By 1850, the original colony had been divided into five territorial divisions. From 1788 to 1824, New South Wales and Van Diemen's Land covered the eastern half of the country and the remaining area was unattached. In 1825, the original colony was extended to 129° longitude and in 1829, the rest of the continent became Western Australia when Perth was settled. In 1836, South Australia was proclaimed a free colony and in 1851 Victoria gained its independence from New South Wales. The final major change occurred when Queensland separated from New South Wales in 1859.

Above: *In recent times, cruising down the Darling River has become a popular holiday trip and an opportunity to experience what was once a vital form of 19th-century transport.*

During this time, the continent was extensively explored, with settlers and adventurers penetrating the interior and discovering vast tracts of excellent grazing land which led to rapid settlement of the region beyond the Great Dividing Range.

The Discovery of Gold

The society changed dramatically in 1851 with the discovery of gold in New South Wales. This was followed by further discoveries in Victoria, Western Australia and Queensland. It was during this time that Sydney and Melbourne became booming metropolitan areas buoyed by the wealth which poured into them from the goldfields.

The impact the Victorian gold rushes had on the state was remarkable. Rural labourers simply downed tools and headed for the goldfields. Transportation and tools were sold at exorbitant rates. Ships from Europe, Asia and the goldfields of California brought tens of thousands of prospectors to the state causing the population to increase from 80,000 in 1851 to 300,000 three years later.

Once the flurry of activity from the gold rushes had subsided the country settled down and in the late 19th century the wealth of the goldfields began to convert itself into vast riches derived from sheep, cattle and wheat industries, the development of other industries and the discovery of minerals other than gold.

GOLD FEVER

Veteran Californian goldminer, Edward Hargraves, first discovered gold near Bathurst in NSW in February 1851. This was quickly followed by gold strikes in Victoria, particularly at Ballarat, one of the largest-ever discoveries. Hopefuls soon poured into the new goldfields from Australia, China, Ireland, North America, England and Europe, although violent opposition to the Chinese sparked race riots. As a result, the population of Victoria increased dramatically and Melbourne rapidly became the largest and wealthiest city in Australia. The gold rushes continued until the end of the century with major discoveries in Western Australia and Queensland in the 1870s and 1880s.

Federation

For at least a decade prior to 1 January 1901, politicians argued the merits of federation. The states had developed their own laws and government procedures and they were unwilling to forsake these powers for some poorly understood concept of a federation which would represent all of Australia. However, the new Commonwealth Parliament was formally opened in Melbourne in 1901 and the seat of power was eventually moved to Canberra. The site had been chosen as early as 1908, but it was not until 1927 that the Federal Parliament began to sit regularly in the newly created city of Canberra.

RELIGIOUS AUSTRALIA

Since 1933, the Australian census form has made it clear that answers to religious affiliation are not obligatory.

By 1986, 25% of the population either reported no religion or did not respond. 73% declared themselves Christian, down from 86.2% in 1971. Of these 26.1% were Catholic, 23.9% Anglican (the latter outnumbered the former in 1971), 7.6% Uniting Church and Methodist, 3.6% Presbyterian and 2.7% Orthodox.

The non-Christian faiths rose from 0.8% in 1971 to 2.0% in 1986 when 0.7% responded Muslim, 0.5% Buddhist and 0.4% Jewish.

The 20th Century

The history of Australia in the 20th century has been a mixture of huge success with the production and international sale of primary products, the deep scars left by two World Wars and the Vietnam war, the debate over a national identity and culture, and the emergence of the country as a significant force in the British Commonwealth and the South-East Asia and Pacific regions.

Federation may have occurred in 1901, but the disparate group of states really had no common identity. It is worth remembering that, without modern transport, the people in Perth and Sydney were days away from each other and, apart from a common Anglo-Saxon background, had little in common. They were as far apart as London was from Athens.

The great defining moment for Australia and the Australian character occurred on 25 April 1915, when a brigade of the AIF (Australian Imperial Force) landed at Anzac Cove, Gallipoli. Nine months later troops were evacuated, but 7,594 Australians had been killed and another 19,500 wounded. It had been a disastrous campaign but the image of the brave, bronzed Australian prepared to fight against the odds and to laugh at authority had been born.

The courage Australian soldiers showed in World War I was once again in evidence in World War II, but this time not only

Left: *The Blue Mountains to the west of Sydney are a world of sheer cliff faces, spectacular views, delightful bushwalks and intimate waterfalls such as these in the Valley of the Waters.*
Opposite: *Most Australians live in cities. However, the image of Australia as a land of hardy rural workers persists. This sheep mustering is taking place in the New England ranges in northern New South Wales.*

were they fighting in Europe and North Africa but also to protect their own country from invasion by Japanese forces which had island-hopped from Japan to the Philippines, Singapore and the Dutch East Indies, and were carrying out bombing raids on the northern coastline and pushing down through Papua New Guinea.

The fear of invasion, partly produced by the vast empty areas of the continent and the rather simple notion that millions of people from Asia would slide down the map and arrive at the northern coast, dictated Australia's foreign policy until the 1980s.

This policy was largely responsible for Australia's involvement in the Korean and Vietnam wars, the country's willing alliance with the USA, and the belief that there was a need to be eternally vigilant.

Modern Multicultural Australia

It has only been in the last few decades that Australia, which until the 1950s was an entirely Anglo-Saxon culture imposed upon a local indigenous population, has started to become multicultural.

The arrival of over a million Italians and a million Greeks in the 20 years after World War II and, more recently, of many Asian people has helped to change attitudes and greatly improve the rather dour British cuisine which dominated throughout the country. The recognition that the world to the north of Australia was

Multicultural Australia

As a result of the progressive removal of immigration restrictions based on race, colour and country of origin, plus the extension to non-British groups and refugees of assisted migration schemes, immigration rates greatly increased in the years after World War II, reaching a peak of 185,000 in 1969–70. After that there was a steady decline to a low of 53,000 in 1975–76, then it began to increase again.

In 1991, 116,650 permanent immigrants were admitted:16.2% were from the UK and Ireland, 12.4% from Hong Kong, 9.2% from Vietnam, 5.7% from New Zealand, 5.5% from the Philippines, 5.5% from India, 3.8% from Malaysia, 2.9% from China, and 2% from Lebanon.

ETHNIC AUSTRALIA

By 1947, 90.2% of the population was born in Australia, up from 77.1% in 1900. A further 7.7% were born in New Zealand or the UK. Changes in immigration policy meant that those born in other countries had increased from 2.1% in 1947 to 14% in 1991. Europe still provides the largest number of foreign-born Australians, but the mixture is changing. Vietnam is the major Asian contributor. In 1991, 7.1% of the population were born in the UK, 1.7% in New Zealand, 1.5% in Italy and 1% in Yugoslavia.

likely to become the economic engine room of the 21st century, made the country aware that it was the only European country in Asia.

As a result, Australia has become a much more interesting and exciting country than it was 50 years ago. It is diverse, multicultural, and eager to face new challenges and opportunities. It is, by most measures, an affluent and successful society.

GOVERNMENT AND ECONOMY

Although the last decade has seen a growing interest in Australia becoming a republic, the country is still a federal parliamentary state presided over by a **constitutional monarchy**. What this means, in practical terms, is that the government and legal system of the country is closely modelled on the British form of government and that Australia still has the British monarch as the head of state.

Each state has a **governor** who is the British monarch's official representative and whose primary functions, apart from attending numerous formal occasions, are to open parliament, to swear-in ministries, and to sign legislation into law. The federal equivalent is the **governor general**. Although generally regarded as a symbolic role (similar in status to the British monarch) all Australians recall the events of 1975, when the governor general of the time, **Sir John Kerr**, sacked Prime Minister **Gough Whitlam** and his government. This exercise of power was an exceptional event which caused considerable controversy. It is unlikely that such action will be taken again.

Australia has three tiers of government: federal, state and local. In practical terms, this division means that the **federal government** is concerned with national issues and thus is in charge of the military forces, aviation,

Below: *In 1988, a superb new Parliament House was built on Canberra's Capital Hill overlooking Lake Burley Griffin. The view from the War Memorial on the other side of the lake is dramatic and gracious.*

diplomatic relations with other countries, national health policies, taxation, customs, industry, transport and communications, trade, resources, social security and similar areas of legislation and jurisdiction. The federal parliament, like its British blueprint, is divided into an upper house (**the Senate**) and a lower house (**the House of Representatives**).

The Senate was originally created to give equal representation to the states. Thus, although there are huge population discrepancies between, say, New South Wales and Tasmania, both states are represented by 12 elected members. In recent times, the Northern Territory and the Australian Capital Territory have each been represented by two Senate members. Senators are elected for six-year terms.

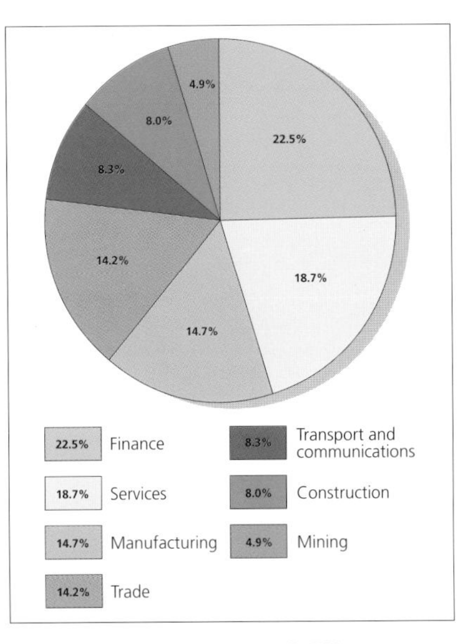

1991–92 GDP FIGURES

The primary function of the Senate, like the House of Lords, is that of a house of review. It critically evaluates legislation from the House of Representatives and makes suggestions and amendments. In recent times it has been difficult for either of the country's major political parties – the **Australian Labor Party** and the **Liberal Party of Australia** – to achieve an absolute majority in the Senate. This has meant that minority parties have been major forces in policy creation.

In spite of the importance of the Senate, the House of Representatives is still the engine room of federal politics. The **prime minister** is a member of the House of Representatives and, because each member is chosen from electorates which are roughly equal in their number of voters, there is a belief that this is the house which truly represents the wishes of Australians. The House of Representatives is re-elected every three years although it is the prime minister's prerogative to call an election.

SOCIAL INDICATORS

- The birth rate in Australia is 15.1 per 1000 (world av. 26.4) and the death rate 7.1 (world av. 9.2).
- The life expectancy for men is 74.4 years and 80.3 years for women. Heart disease is the major cause of death.
- Of those aged between 15 and 69 only 0.3% have no formal schooling and 43.6% have some sort of post-secondary qualification.
- The average working week is 40.1 hours and the average weekly earnings in 1992 were A$507.90.
- 92% of dwellings have a flush toilet, while 86% of households possess an automobile and 10.1% a swimming pool.

AUSTRALIA'S BALANCE OF PAYMENTS

In 1991–92 the revenue of the Australian government was A$99 billion and expenditure A$115 billion.
- 68.9% of revenue was from income tax (51.1% individual and 17.8% corporate) and 23.5% from sales and excise taxes.
- 34.2% of expenditure was on social security and welfare; 25.2% on transfers to state governments; 9.1% on transfers to the non-budget sector; and 5.6% on the interest on public debt.

Each state has a similar bicameral arrangement. The notable exception is Queensland, where the Upper House was abandoned, reflecting the widely held perception that, at state government level, the Upper House is a rather attractive sinecure for political worthies and has little effective power.

There are significant variations in voting behaviour and legislative process between states. However, the most common arrangement is for elections to be called every three years. The government is then constituted from the party with the largest number of representatives.

State governments are primarily concerned with state issues. Their major areas of legislative and administrative interest are education, the police force, roads, hospitals and local health.

The most grassroots of all the political forms is **local government**. There are thousands of local councils throughout Australia. Most are run by councillors who receive a small stipend and who make decisions about local roads, sewerage, rubbish collection, planning permission and property development in the local district. They are often constrained by state and federal legislation but they do enjoy considerable power within their local community.

Below: *Red river gums by a creek or river are a natural part of Australia's rural beauty. These gums in South Australia's Flinders Ranges are reflected in the waters of a small creek.*

The Economy

Like most countries in the western world, Australia went through a lengthy recession in the late 1980s and only began to re-emerge into economic prosperity in 1994. Part of Australia's problem was that, even in the 1980s and 1990s, the economy was largely dependent on the export of primary products and this sector of the economy was vulnerable to fluctuations in world commodity prices and the healthiness of overseas economies.

In recent years, Australia has focused its attentions on South-East Asia and become an important supplier to the region's manufacturing industries. It is significant that the traditional trade relationship between Australia and the UK has now shrunk to a point where it is smaller than that with Singapore.

Nearly 50% of the country's wealth was derived from mineral fuels and crude materials such as ores, scrap metal and textile fibres. These raw materials provide most of the country's residents with a good standard of living. Literacy is at 99.5%, average household income is A$33,100 and the daily calorie intake is 124% of the recommended minimum requirement.

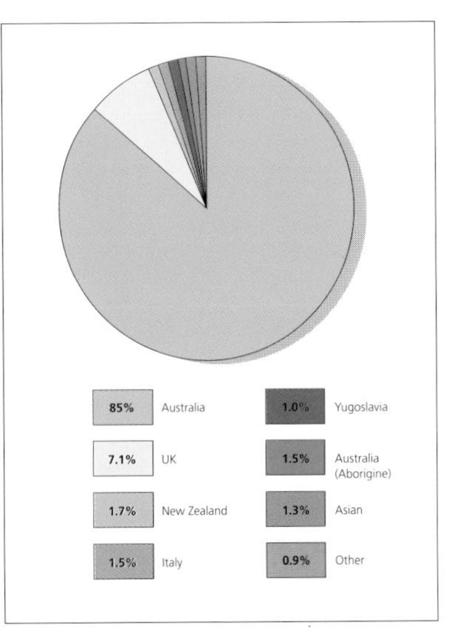

POPULATION CHART BY COUNTRY OF BIRTH

THE PEOPLE

Australians are basically gregarious, informal people. Overseas visitors often comment on the willingness of Australians to stop and help a traveller who appears lost, the ready smiles which seem to accompany everyday discourse, and the casual way Australians deal with business activities.

Visitors used to societies which are aggressively driven by customer service will often find that Australian service, particularly in shops, hotels and in the tourist trade, is lax and informal. Australians do not like to see themselves as aggressive. This may come as a surprise to visitors who find that the linguistic tendency to finish a sentence on a rising note sounds abrasive and questioning.

It is important to remember the roots of Australian society. The European community in Australia was almost totally Anglo-Saxon until the 1950s. The resistance to overseas and multicultural impulses was strong. There was, for nearly a century, an informal policy which was dubbed '**the White Australia Policy**' which made entry into the country for non-Anglo-Saxons nearly impossible.

It is also important to recognise that most Australians are proud of the country's convict heritage. Jokes about the society being a collection of descendants of convicts are now totally inaccurate. However, they can be rebutted by proud declarations that Australia is a very egalitarian society (there is only a very small 'upper class' and they are not widely admired) which is based on personal success and whether or not you are a decent and worthwhile human being. Australians dislike people who achieve and then

Right: *Multicultural Australia is about drinking cappuccino, eating Thai food, worshipping in a mosque or, like these children in Dutch costume, admiring tulips at a flower farm in Victoria's Dandenong Range.*
Opposite: *One of South Australia's most unusual tourist attractions is the Blue Lake at Mount Gambier. In November this incredibly deep volcanic lake turns a deep blue. It reverts to grey in May–June. There is no known explanation for the phenomenon.*

brashly display their new-found wealth and status. This has been dubbed 'the tall poppy syndrome'. It means that there is a great acceptance of achievement matched with humility and a great intolerance of achievement when it is associated with flashy vulgarity.

Similarly, the country still perceives a deep division between 'workers' and 'bosses'. One theory argues that these feelings date back to convict times when relationships between convicts and overseers were similarly antagonistic.

Living in the City

85% of Australians live in urban areas and almost two-thirds of the population live in the state capitals. In 1993, only 11 Australian cities had over 100,000 inhabitants:
Sydney, NSW – 3,719,000
Melbourne, Vic – 3,187,500
Brisbane, Qld – 1,421,700
Adelaide, SA – 1,070,200
Newcastle, NSW – 455,700
Canberra, ACT – 325,700
Gold Coast, Qld – 300,200
Wollongong, NSW – 250,000
Hobart, Tas – 193,300
Geelong, Vic – 151,800
Townsville, Qld – 121,700

The Multicultural Mix

After World War II Australia embarked on an active immigration programme. The result of this rapid cultural mix was a huge change in lifestyle. It is hard to imagine that in the early 1950s the average Australian would never have eaten pasta, rarely drunk coffee, probably never bought a bottle of wine and regarded all non-British people as dirty and dangerous.

Today, Australia (particularly the cities) is a truly multicultural society. The average Australian delights in the variety of cuisine available. Thai, Vietnamese, Chinese and Italian restaurants abound, outdoor cafés capitalising on the sunny weather are commonplace, international clothing is popular, and the learning of non-traditional, non-European languages – particularly Japanese and Indonesian – has increased dramatically in schools.

The Aboriginal Society

It is easy when discussing Australian society to ignore the original inhabitants. In recent times Aborigines, who for most of the country's European history had been treated appallingly, have asserted their rights. This hardly redresses the long period of imbalance when they were poisoned, massacred, driven from their land, forced into reserves, treated as social outcasts and had their families torn apart.

Aborigines currently account for 1.5% of the country's population. With a few notable exceptions they live in sub-standard conditions which are characterised by disproportionate levels of unemployment, crime and imprisonment.

The country's Aboriginal and Torres Strait Islander population has been slowly increasing over the past two decades. This may be because more part-Aborigines are registering themselves as Aborigines. It may also be because government programmes are having an effect on lifespan and infant mortality levels. In 1971, there were 115,953 Aborigines registered. This had increased to 265,492 by 1991. Two-thirds of this population live in Queensland, the Northern Territory and Western Australia.

ABORIGINAL POPULATION

It has been estimated that the Aboriginal population in 1788 was 300,000–500,000

Year	Population
1860	22,000
1901	93,000
1911	80,000
1921	72,000
1933	81,000
1947	76,000
1961	84,500
1971	116,000
1981	160,000
1991	265,000

The decline in population is due to introduced diseases, brutality, dispossession and massacres. Its recent increase reflects greater expenditure on welfare and health.

Aboriginal Culture

Aboriginal culture is as sophisticated as its technology is simple. Complex ceremonies fusing song, dance, body painting, religion, history and behavioural prescriptions express the lore of the Dreamtime. This embodies the eternal presence, the activities and the unpredictable influence of the beings who were the creators of all things, and the laws relating to interaction with each other and the land. They also tell where to hunt, the location of food and water, and ideal marriage partners.

'**Sacred sites**' are of great significance. They are portions of the landscape which are regarded as incarnations of Dreamtime ancestors.

In recent years major changes have occurred and the conditions of some Aborigines have improved. Perhaps most significantly in 1994 the federal government converted the high court's '**Mabo**' decision into legislation. This legislation stated that if Aborigines could prove continuous connection with the land they could, under most circumstances, claim that land as their own. This reversed the famous *terra nullius* proposition which was created when Captain Cook stood at Cape York and, in spite of seeing obvious signs of human inhabitation, declared that Australia was uninhabited and, therefore, could legitimately be claimed by the British crown.

Aboriginal Culture

Aboriginal (**Koori**) culture preceded the arrival of Europeans by at least 40,000 years; a period in which it developed in almost complete isolation.

Vital to indigenous culture are the **Dreamtime** stories concerning the creation and history of the land and its people. Every individual is regarded as a descendant of something in nature, as a part of the spirit which inhabits the land.

Prior to European settlement there were many hundreds of groups with different languages and practices. They lived in relative harmony due to their shared belief in their oneness with the land, which was thought to have been allotted to each tribe in the Dreamtime. The groups traded with each other but maintained and protected their own sacred sites which were taboo to outsiders. There were elders but no chiefs. Laws concerning behaviour were strictly enforced. Men hunted and fished while women collected seeds and roots. Most implements were made of wood. There is evidence of the use of stone tools 10,000 years before they were being used in Europe. Painting, music and dance rituals were integral to everyday life.

When Europeans arrived, the progressive destruction of Aboriginal culture began. Only recently has the problem received attention and some belated understanding.

Australian Culture

Australian cultural life has changed dramatically over the past 50 years. From a narrow cultural world which was based on the proposition that everything from the UK was good and everything that existed in Australia was second-rate, there has been a growing sense of national pride. Today Australians are proud of their multicultural society where differences are accepted.

Left: *The beautiful Atherton Tablelands behind Cairns in north Queensland are noted for the dense tropical rainforests and waterfalls. It is said that during the rainy season, when the Millstream Falls near Ravenshoe are in flood, they are the widest falls in Australia.*

There is still a tendency to take great pride in overseas recognition. Thus **Patrick White** (who won the Nobel Prize for Literature) and **Thomas Keneally** and **Peter Carey** (who both have won the Booker Prize) are lionized as the country's greatest writers.

Australian films and their makers have also been successful. **Jane Campion**'s *The Piano*, **Scott Hicks**'s *Shine* and **Baz Luhrmann**'s *Strictly Ballroom* and *Romeo and Juliet* have all achieved international recognition and the odd Academy or Golden Globe Award. Cinematographer **Dean Semmler** won an 'Oscar' for *Dances with Wolves*, and directors **Peter Weir**, **Fred Schepsi** and **Bruce Beresford** have all been nominated. Perhaps Australia's biggest successes are actor/director **Mel Gibson** and actress **Nicole Kidman**.

The country has a healthy art scene with orchestras of international standing, opera singers starring in the world's great opera houses, ballet dancers and dance troupes receiving international acclaim, and painters and artists (notably the late **Sidney Nolan**) who are represented in the world's great art collections and galleries.

National Symbols

The Australian coat of arms consists of a shield in six parts, each containing a state badge. The ermine border around them represents their federation within a national umbrella. It is supported by two typically Australian animals, the emu and the kangaroo. Behind them is a representative Australian plant, the wattle. The crest, a seven-pointed Commonwealth gold star, is a symbol of national unity.

The Australian national anthem is 'Advance Australia Fair'. The first and last four bars are used in the presence of the governor general while 'God Save the Queen' is still used in the presence of the British Queen. There is an on-going debate about changing the country's flag and national anthem.

Of course the day-to-day cultural reality for the average Australian is markedly different. The obsessive love of sport, the fascination with television, the unswerving desire to go to pubs, go on picnics, and have a good time outdoors, are still the most vital features of the country's culture. The notion that this is somehow unique to Australia is nonsense. It is just that Australia's working class spreads far into the middle class and thus working-class cultural values – built around sport, recreation and leisure – tend to dominate.

Sport and Recreation

Unlike most countries Australia does not have a large number of national sports. In winter, rugby union and rugby league are played in Queensland and New South Wales; Australian rules in South Australia, Western Australia and Tasmania; and soccer is played throughout the country. The summer sports of cricket, tennis and swimming tend to be nationwide, although the eastern states are more enthusiastic and often win the major competitions such as cricket's Sheffield Shield.

The strength of Australian sport lies more in the number of people who play it rather than in the number of people who watch it. On any Saturday, in any reasonably sized town or suburb, there will be competitions at the local tennis courts, golf courses, netball courts, and the cricket and football fields. There is also a large amount of purely recreational fishing, bushwalking,

CURRENCY

Depicted on Australia's currency are the echidna (5c), five kangaroos (A$1), an Australian Aborigine (A$2), poets Mary Gilmore and 'Banjo' Paterson (A$10), Mary Reibey and John Flynn, (A$20), David Unaipon and Edith Cowan (A$50), and on the A$100 note, soprano opera singer, Dame Nellie Melba, and soldier and engineer, Sir John Monash.

swimming (at beaches, local council swimming pools and rivers), and it is very common for outdoor picnics and barbecues to be accompanied by a friendly game of touch football, French cricket or some similarly energetic sport.

Of course, all this enthusiasm in part led to Australia's success in the 1996 Atlanta Olympic Games, where the national team won more medals per capita than any other country competing. This is a grand lead-up to Sydney hosting the 2000 Olympics, where it is hoped that Australian achievements will be even more impressive!

Food and Drink

There was a time when breakfast consisted of steak, fried tomatoes and eggs. Equally, there was a time when a social lunchtime would ensure that the barbecue would be lit and sausages, steaks and onions would be cooked. The accompanying tomato sauce, bread and butter, green salad with no dressing and perhaps a rice salad (all washed down with beer for the men and shandies or wine for the women) were part of the fabric of Australian weekend entertainment.

While all of these activities are still common, the concern about calorie intake and the increasing variety of foods available as a result of the country's multicultural make-up, have meant that these clichés no longer apply.

It is quite likely that beer at the barbecue has been replaced by a fine wine from the Hunter Valley, the Barossa Valley or the Margaret River area of Western Australia. The sauces may well have given way to something more exotic from Asia, and prawns (shrimp), pieces of fish and chicken are replacing the heavier red meats.

Australians eat and drink well. They are able to do so because they have a high standard of living and because the produce of the country is of a high quality, is readily available and is, by world standards, very cheap.

Overseas visitors quite often gasp in disbelief when they visit a restaurant and find that their bill is less than half what they would pay at home and the food – notable for its freshness – has been better than they could buy in their own country.

Gum Trees

One thing that strikes every visitor to Australia is the country's seemingly endless forests of gum trees. They are common in suburban gardens, they grow anywhere the land hasn't been cleared, they are easily ignited and consequently are nearly always at the centre of bushfires. They can look grey; on the east coast they can look blue when a fine eucalypt mist rises from them. They are Australia's most distinctive symbol and are a characteristic feature of Australian art.

There are around 700 species of eucalypt, almost all of which occur naturally in Australia. In fact 75% of Australian trees are gums. They range in size and shape from the bush-like mallee and the truncated, gnarled and colourfully streaked snow gums to the jarrah and karri forest giants of Western Australia and the mountain ash of Tasmania and Victoria. They are the tallest flowering plants in the world, attaining heights of 100m (328ft). The fragrant oil of the eucalypt is used in flavourings and pharmaceuticals, the wood often makes excellent timber and its leaves are virtually the sole diet of koalas.

Opposite: *The Australian love of sun, sand and sport finds perfect expression with this social game of volleyball on Sydney's famous Manly Beach.*

AMP

2
Sydney and New South Wales

State car number-plates declare 'New South Wales – The Premier State'. In one sense it simply means 'The First State' but in another it means 'The Best State'– the state whose capital city is regarded as one of the most beautiful cities in the world.

The truth is that, while Sydney remains the oldest and largest city in Australia, the state continues to enjoy its 'premier' position. It is, by any definition, a remarkable city. Starting over 200 years ago as a penal colony at the end of the earth, it has dragged itself up by the bootstraps. The beauty of its setting and the mildness of its climate make it a near-perfect place to live.

The beauty of New South Wales extends beyond simply having Sydney as its capital. Although it takes up only 10% of Australia it has a diversity of landform, climate and vegetation which is richer and more complex than any other state, with tropical rainforests in the north, Alpine ski slopes in the south, seemingly endless beaches on the east coast and deserts in the west.

Don't Miss in Sydney

*** **Sydney Tower**: Sydney's tallest building has magnificent views and houses three restaurants. One is for private functions while the other two are open for lunch and evening meals.
** **Sydney Harbour Bridge**: views of the harbour are available from the south-east pylon which is open between 10:00 and 17:00 daily. It is also possible to walk across the bridge to North Sydney.

Sydney

All explorations of New South Wales, indeed all explorations of Australia, must start with Sydney. It is a city of mild temperatures, of evenly distributed rainfall with slight maximums in the late autumn and early winter, and glorious, balmy, subtropical summer days of sunshine with people sunning themselves on the necklace of beaches which spread to the north and the south of the harbour.

Opposite: *Designed by the Danish architect Jørn Utzon, the Sydney Opera House, with its white sails, has become the most recognised symbol of Australia.*

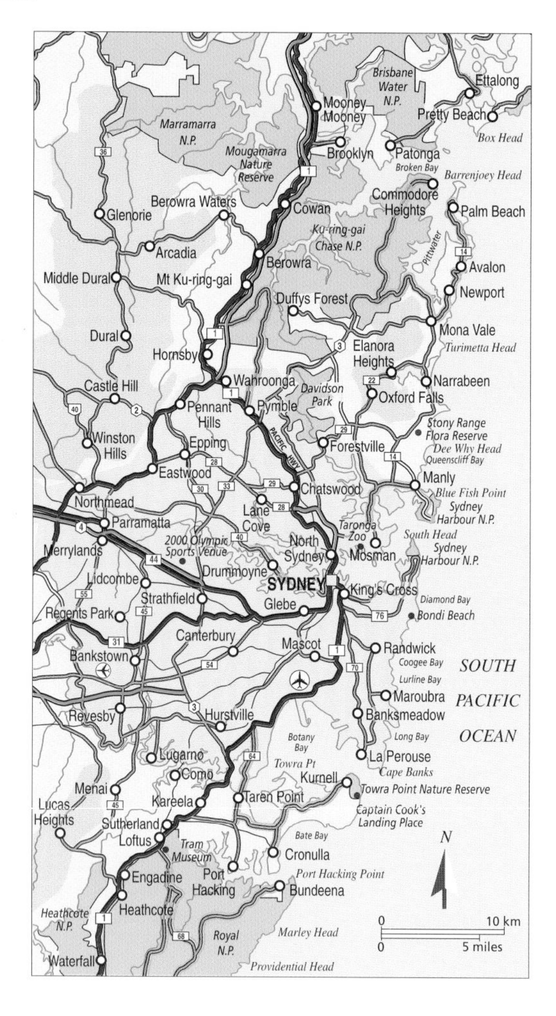

The cityscape has two monuments: the Sydney Harbour Bridge and the Opera House which mirrors the sails of the yachts racing across the harbour at the weekends.

Sydney started its life as a penal colony. Its first European inhabitants were mostly either soldiers or criminals. Its harbour also became a port where sailors took shore leave, looking for cheap thrills to balance the monotony of life at sea. To appreciate the history of the city, visitors should head towards The Rocks.

City Sightseeing

A good place to start your exploration of Sydney is **The Rocks.** Although it has now become a series of pubs, restaurants and shops for tourists, it is still possible to see that, in the 18th century, this was the centre of the city's wild military and convict nightlife. When **Circular Quay** was the city's port, the area's solid Victorian sandstone buildings functioned as warehouses. Move east along Circular Quay towards the Opera House and you can catch a ferry across the harbour. The short trip across to **McMahons Point** affords excellent views of the Opera House, passes under the Harbour Bridge, and lands the visitor at the bottom of a hill which leads up to North Sydney, the city's centre of computer technology and advertising.

The ferry service to **Parramatta** takes passengers west until the harbour is reduced to a narrow river.

Widely recognised as the two best ferry trips are those to **Taronga Zoo** and to **Manly**. The zoo is beautifully located on the slopes overlooking the harbour, and beyond it is Athol Park which offers delightful walks through bushland. On the trip across to Manly the ferry passes North and South heads and provides many spectacular views of the harbour. On a par with Bondi, Manly is Sydney's most famous beach. A short walk along The Corso will take the visitor from the harbourside ferry terminus to the ocean beach.

Beyond Circular Quay is the world-famous **Sydney Opera House**, which has excellent views of the Quay and the Harbour Bridge as well as containing a range of restaurants and coffee shops. The Opera House's numerous theatres range from small drama spaces to concert halls and the main opera theatre itself.

CLIMATE

Sydneysiders feel that they live in a city with a perfect climate. The summers are usually long and sunny. It is, however, common to have summer storms and the city's famous 'southerly buster' – a dramatic cold change often after particularly hot and humid days – is a feature of those hot summer days which sends temperatures tumbling. The winters are mild, and spring and autumn are typically balmy.

Left: *Built between 1923 and 1932, and one of the largest single-span bridges in the world, the Sydney Harbour Bridge is the premier icon of Sydney. Known as 'The Coat-Hanger' or simply 'The Bridge', the main span is 503m (1659ft) long and the top of the arch is 134m (440ft) above sea level.*

Taronga Zoo

Voted the best international zoo in 1992, Taronga Zoo has superb views of Sydney Harbour and a substantial collection of Australian native fauna. The zoo can be reached by ferry from Wharf 2, Circular Quay (the journey takes 12 minutes) or by bus from Wynyard or St Leonards.

Open from 09:00 to 17:00 every day of the year the displays include echidnas, dingoes, wombats, kangaroos and wallabies, Australian snakes and spiders. The koala walkabout and platypus exhibit offer exceptional vantage points of the city.

To the east of the Opera House lie the city's **Botanic Gardens** and **Lady Macquarie's Chair**, where the wife of one of the colony's early governors used to sit and enjoy the view across the harbour.

Returning to The Rocks the visitor now heads west. Travelling underneath the Harbour Bridge one passes the old waterfront wharves on the way to **Darling Harbour**.

This is Sydney's equivalent to Fisherman's Wharf in San Francisco. It is a large complex of shops, restaurants and modestly-priced eateries, all set against a backdrop of the harbour. Situated at the northern end is the **Sydney Aquarium**, showcasing Australia's aquatic life. At the southern end lies the **Chinese Gardens**, reputedly the largest of its type outside China.

From Darling Harbour the visitor can take the **monorail** into the central business district where department and specialist stores offer a wide range of goods. Most of the major stores have duty-free facilities for tourists.

Eating out

Just beyond Darling Harbour is Sydney's **Chinatown**. The Chinese settled in Australia during the gold rushes of the 1850s. More recently, large numbers of Asians, many of them refugees from Indo-China, have arrived. Chinatown offers a wide range of Asian cuisine from Vietnam and Thailand, as well as regional varieties of Chinese cooking.

Right: *Sydney is much more than just another modern city of high-rise buildings. Its unique position on one of the world's great natural harbours, and its inviting subtropical parks such as the Botanic Gardens, offer visitors hours of enjoyable scenic walks.*

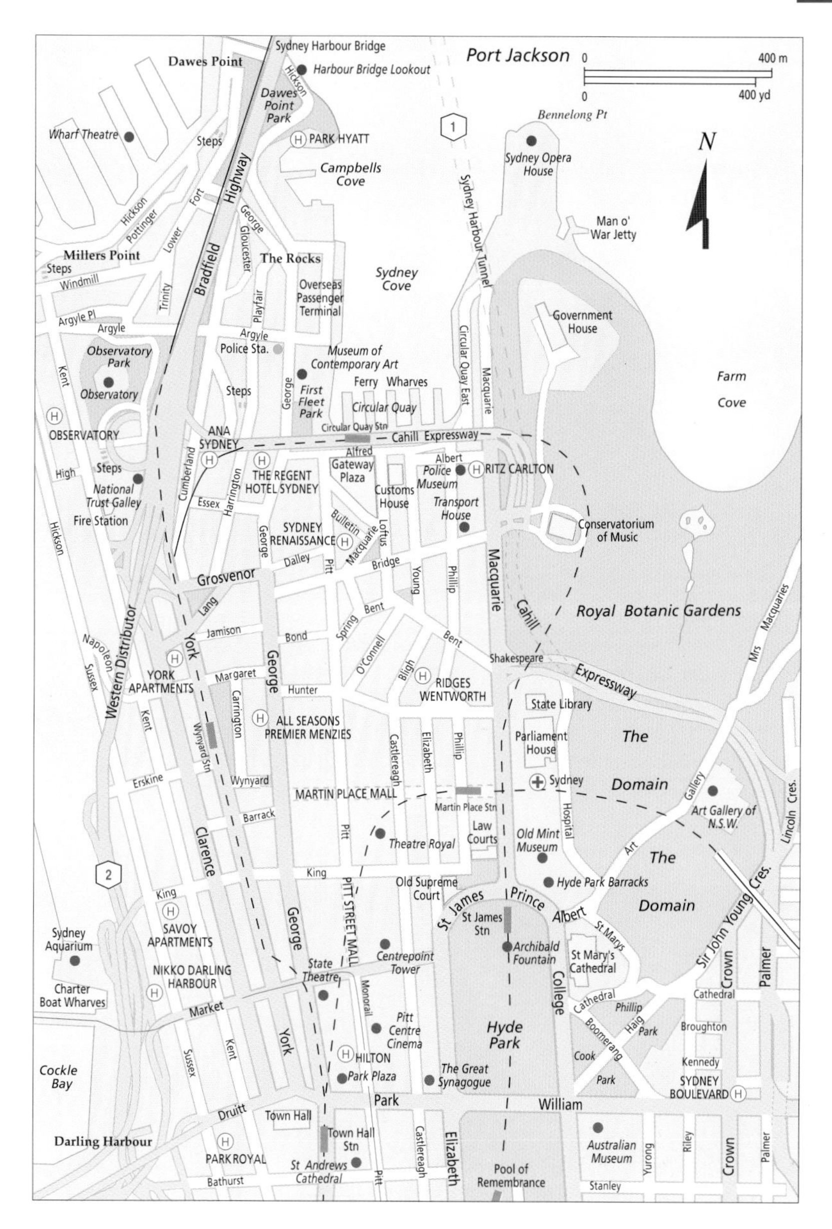
Port Jackson
0 400 m
0 400 yd
N
Sydney Harbour Bridge
Dawes Point
Harbour Bridge Lookout
Dawes Point Park
Wharf Theatre
Steps
PARK HYATT
Campbells Cove
Bennelong Pt
Sydney Opera House
Sydney Harbour Tunnel
Man o' War Jetty
Bradfield Highway
Hickson
Pottinger
Lower
Fort
George
Gloucester
Millers Point
The Rocks
Windmill
Trinity
Playfair
Overseas Passenger Terminal
Sydney Cove
Government House
Argyle Pl
Argyle
Observatory Park
Observatory
Police Sta.
Museum of Contemporary Art
Ferry Wharves
Circular Quay East
Macquarie
Farm Cove
Kent
First Fleet Park
Circular Quay
OBSERVATORY
ANA SYDNEY
Circular Quay Stn
Cahill Expressway
High
Steps
National Trust Gallery
Fire Station
Cumberland
Essex
Harrington
THE REGENT HOTEL SYDNEY
Alfred
Gateway Plaza
Customs House
Albert
Police Museum
RITZ CARLTON
Transport House
Conservatorium of Music
Hickson
SYDNEY RENAISSANCE
Bulletin
Macquarie
Loftus
Dalley
Pitt
Bridge
Young
Phillip
Grosvenor
Lang
Cahill
Royal Botanic Gardens
Mrs Macquaries
Western Distributor
Napoleon
Sussex
York
Jamison
Bond
Spring
Bent
O'Connell
Bent
Shakespeare
Expressway
YORK APARTMENTS
Margaret
Carrington
George
Hunter
Bligh
RIDGES WENTWORTH
State Library
ALL SEASONS PREMIER MENZIES
Wynyard Stn
Castlereagh
Elizabeth
Phillip
Parliament House
The Domain
Erskine
Wynyard
MARTIN PLACE MALL
Sydney
Martin Place Stn
Hospital
Gallery
Art Gallery of N.S.W.
Lincoln Cres.
Barrack
Clarence
Pitt
Law Courts
Theatre Royal
Old Mint Museum
Art
The Domain
2
King
Hyde Park Barracks
Old Supreme Court
St James
Prince Albert
Sir John Young Cres.
King
SAVOY APARTMENTS
PITT STREET MALL
St James Stn
St Marys
Sydney Aquarium
Archibald Fountain
St Mary's Cathedral
Crown
Palmer
NIKKO DARLING HARBOUR
Centrepoint Tower
State Theatre
College
Charter Boat Wharves
Market
Monorail
Cathedral
Phillip
Cathedral
Pitt Centre Cinema
Hyde Park
Boomerang
Haig
Park
Broughton
Cockle Bay
Sussex
Kent
York
HILTON
Cook
Kennedy
Park Plaza
The Great Synagogue
Park
SYDNEY BOULEVARD
Park
William
Druitt
Town Hall
Darling Harbour
Town Hall Stn
Castlereagh
Elizabeth
Australian Museum
Yurong
Riley
Crown
Palmer
PARKROYAL
St Andrews Cathedral
Pitt
Pool of Remembrance
Bathurst
Stanley

Open-air Markets

Sydney has a number of excellent outdoor markets. The most famous is **Paddy's Market** at Haymarket. Originally a fruit and vegetable market it has expanded to include a wide variety of goods and gifts.

A popular haunt is the **'Paddo' Bazaar** at 395 Oxford Street. Held each Saturday between 10:00 and 16:00 it offers crafts, foods and handmade garments. Its location on Oxford Street (the centre of Sydney's colourful gay community) ensures that the market is fascinating for those wanting to experience the heart of inner-Sydney living.

Below: *West of Sydney lie the Blue Mountains, a series of box canyons with sheer cliffs, waterfalls and spectacular views. The experience of travelling on the Katoomba Skyway and looking across at the Three Sisters is both magnificent and hair-raising.*

Museums

Behind Darling Harbour is the excellent **Powerhouse Museum**, a science and technology museum which has a variety of interesting hands-on exhibits. On the other side of the city centre is the **Art Gallery of New South Wales**, which offers an excellent overview of Australian art and good collections of international artists. The **Australian Museum** is the nation's oldest and largest natural history museum. Its displays of Australian flora and fauna are considered the finest in the country.

Around Sydney

There are several interesting daytrips to towns and sights which should be considered part of any visit to Sydney. The most spectacular experience within easy reach of Sydney is that offered by the **Blue Mountains**. On a clear day, from high vantage points near the city, it is easy to see the mountains touched with that distinctive smoky blue which rises from the dense stands of eucalypts.

The mountains were not crossed until 1813. By the 1880s they had become a major tourist attraction and a kind of Australian 'hill station' where people could escape Sydney's summer humidity.

Today, the Blue Mountains have a special charm. The air is bracing – in fact it is quite common for **Katoomba** at 1017m (3337ft) above sea level to have snow in winter. In the 1920s and 1930s it was *the* place for a holiday and hotels such as The Carrington at Katoomba, Cooper's Grand Hotel and the Hydro Majestic at Medlow Bath, gained reputations as places for a *risqué* weekend.

With its spectacular views across the Grose and Jamison valleys, Katoomba is the main tourist attraction. Highlights are the **Three Sisters** on the edge of the Jamison Valley, the

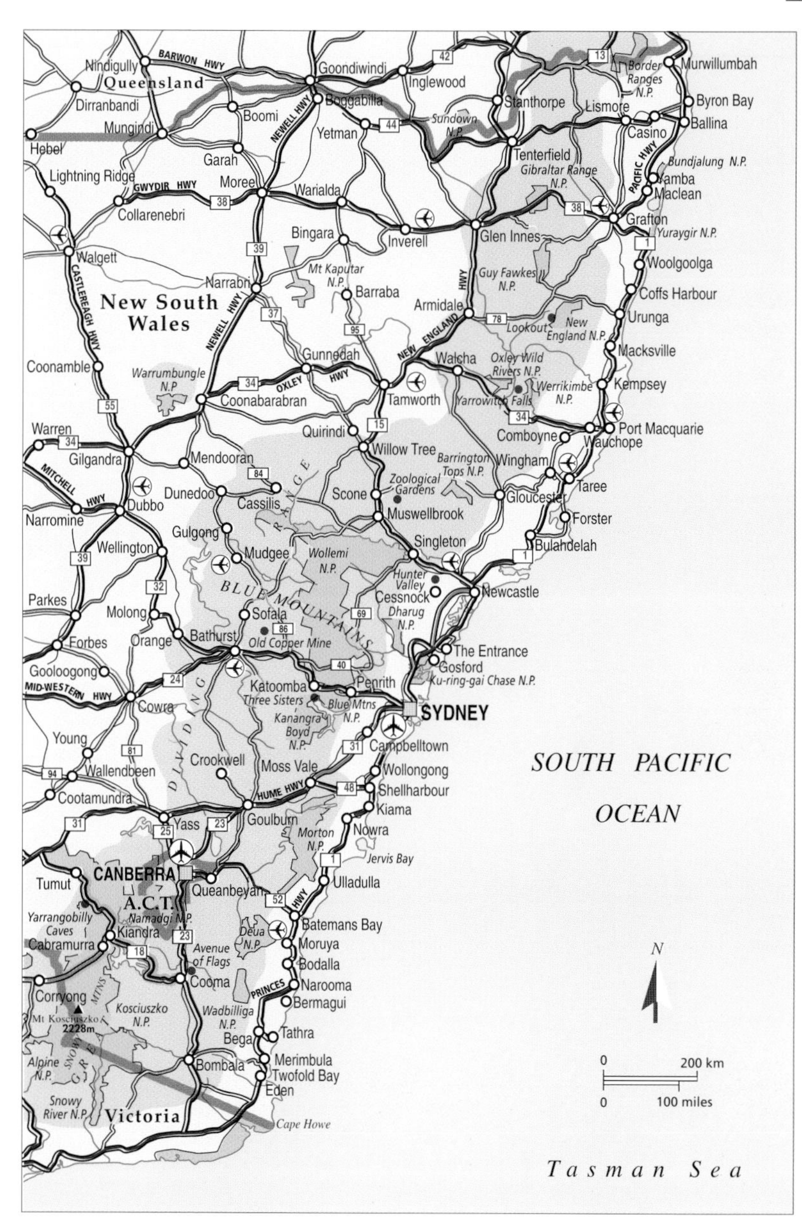

Queensland
New South Wales
Victoria
A.C.T.
SOUTH PACIFIC OCEAN
Tasman Sea
SYDNEY
CANBERRA
BLUE MOUNTAINS
DIVIDING RANGE
BARWON HWY
GWYDIR HWY
NEWELL HWY
CASTLEREAGH HWY
OXLEY HWY
NEW ENGLAND HWY
PACIFIC HWY
MITCHELL HWY
MID-WESTERN HWY
HUME HWY
PRINCES HWY
Nindigully
Dirranbandi
Mungindi
Hebel
Goondiwindi
Boggabilla
Boomi
Garah
Inglewood
Yetman
Stanthorpe
Sundown N.P.
Lismore
Border Ranges N.P.
Murwillumbah
Byron Bay
Ballina
Casino
Tenterfield
Gibraltar Range N.P.
Bundjalung N.P.
Yamba
Maclean
Grafton
Yuraygir N.P.
Lightning Ridge
Moree
Warialda
Collarenebri
Bingara
Inverell
Glen Innes
Walgett
Mt Kaputar N.P.
Narrabri
Barraba
Guy Fawkes N.P.
Woolgoolga
Coffs Harbour
Urunga
Armidale
Lookout
New England N.P.
Macksville
Gunnedah
Walcha
Oxley Wild Rivers N.P.
Kempsey
Coonamble
Warrumbungle N.P.
Coonabarabran
Tamworth
Yarrowitch Falls
Werrikimbe N.P.
Port Macquarie
Wauchope
Comboyne
Quirindi
Warren
Gilgandra
Willow Tree
Barrington Tops N.P.
Wingham
Mendooran
Zoological Gardens
Taree
Dunedoo
Cassilis
Scone
Gloucester
Narromine
Dubbo
Muswellbrook
Forster
Gulgong
Bulahdelah
Wellington
Mudgee
Wollemi N.P.
Singleton
Hunter Valley
Cessnock
Newcastle
Parkes
Molong
Sofala
Dharug N.P.
Forbes
Orange
Bathurst
Old Copper Mine
The Entrance
Gosford
Ku-ring-gai Chase N.P.
Gooloogong
Katoomba
Penrith
Three Sisters
Blue Mtns N.P.
Cowra
Kanangra Boyd N.P.
Young
Campbelltown
Crookwell
Moss Vale
Wollongong
Wallendbeen
Shellharbour
Cootamundra
Kiama
Yass
Goulburn
Morton N.P.
Nowra
Jervis Bay
Tumut
Queanbeyan
Ulladulla
Yarrangobilly Caves
Namadgi N.P.
Batemans Bay
Kiandra
Cabramurra
Deua N.P.
Moruya
Avenue of Flags
Bodalla
Cooma
Narooma
Corryong
Bermagui
Mt Kosciuszko 2228m
Kosciuszko N.P.
Wadbilliga N.P.
Bega
Tathra
Alpine N.P.
SNOWY MTNS
Bombala
Merimbula
Twofold Bay
Eden
Snowy River N.P.
Cape Howe
N
0 200 km
0 100 miles

Above: *Quaint, old-fashioned cottages cling to the hillside behind Garie Beach.*

waterfall at **Govett's Leap**, the **scenic railway** at Katoomba, Norman Lindsay's home in Springwood, the **Jenolan Caves** and the **Kanangra Walls**. The views are breath-taking, the eating places are quiet and elegant, and the hotels have a special charm.

Another area beloved of Sydney high society prior to World War II was the **Southern Highlands**. The mildness of the weather, particularly the coolness of the summers, attracted the visitors. The area is home to some of the country's finest cattle studs.

Attractions of the area include the **Wombeyan Caves**, the spectacular **Fitzroy Falls**, the well-preserved historic town of **Berrima**, the gracious gardens of **Bowral** (open in late September during Tulip Festival time) and, especially for cricket lovers, the **Don Bradman Museum** in Bowral. The area is dotted with large homes and hotels.

To the east of the Southern Highlands is the beautiful **South Coast**. The traveller leaving Sydney and heading south first comes to the **Royal National Park** which spreads from the beaches of **Wattamolla** and **Garie** through to the quiet waters of the Hacking River. Covering 14,969ha (37,000 acres) this glorious park lies less than 40km (25 miles) from the centre of Sydney and was Australia's first national park.

Visitors to the park can go surfing, lagoon swimming or fishing. They can have a picnic or spend a day rowing or paddling on the small lake above **Audley Weir**. Or they can walk along the hundreds of bush trails which were developed in the park in the 1920s.

Other areas of particular interest around Sydney are the historic Macquarie towns (**Richmond** and **Windsor**) to the west, the holiday resort area of **Gosford**, and the **Hunter Valley**, the most famed wine-growing area in New South Wales.

Eating in the Blue Mountains

The Blue Mountains are famous for unusual and interesting restaurants, many of which have spectacular views. The official guide to the area, *The Blue Mountains Experience* (a free publication), lists dozens of restaurants and cafés. Here is a small selection:

- **The Paragon Café**, Katoomba – famed as a relic of the Australian café of the 1930s.
- **Pegums**, Lawson – renowned as one of the country's finest restaurants.
- **Fairmont Resort**, Leura – good food with breathtaking views across the valley.

The New South Wales Coast

New South Wales' greatest asset is undoubtedly its 1900km (1180 miles) of coastline. Although the coast has only a few natural harbours, it does have vast numbers of superb beaches.

Along the eastern seaboard lies the fertile coastal plain. It is home to the bulk of the state's dairy industry, vegetable production and tropical fruit plantations. Its agriculture shifts from the bananas, macadamias, pineapples and avocados of the north, to the dairy and beef cattle which are typical of the south coast.

The north coast of New South Wales – **Byron Bay**, **Ballina**, **Yamba**, even as far south as **Port Macquarie** – is an area of tourism, dairy and beef cattle, timber cutting and subtropical plantation farming.

Further south is **Newcastle**, the state's second-largest city. Its prosperity is based on its steel industry which, in turn, is based on the substantial coal deposits from the Hunter Valley and the port facilities which allow ships to bring iron-ore to the steelworks for processing. The wine-producing areas are a major tourist attraction, with a wide variety of vineyards offering accommodation, good eating and excellent wines.

South of Newcastle, the **Wyong–Gosford** area, once dominated by the cheap weekenders of Sydneysiders, is now a commuter belt. Soaring Sydney land prices and a fast electric train have helped to convert these one-time holiday retreats into Sydney's northernmost suburbs. The Central Coast now reaches beyond Gosford to Toukley and the Tuggerah Lake, Munmorah Lake and Lake Macquarie regions.

To the south of Sydney, the coastal road from **Stanwell Tops** to **Wollongong** is full of surprises. It starts with one of the most spectacular views on the entire east coast of Australia, moves through a series of old coal-mining villages which cling to the edge of cliffs that drop precipitously to the dark waters of the Pacific, and then continues on to New South Wales' third-largest city – Wollongong.

Wollongong is a mixture of industry and tourism. On one level it is a typical steel town. On another level it is edged by a series of excellent beaches. It is possible to lie on the beach without a care in the world while, over the nearest sand dune, gas flames reach high into the sky.

South of Wollongong, the coastal strip is primarily dairy country. It is still common for the traveller driving along a winding country road to be caught behind a herd of Fresians making their way languidly towards the milking sheds. The valleys of the escarpment, with their spectacular array of waterfalls and ferns, lyrebirds, wallabies

Alternative Lifestyles

In recent years the north coast of New South Wales has become one of the country's most fashionable retreats. It was originally dairy farming land but hippies moved in during the 1960s. The area around **Byron Bay** now attracts media personalities because of its superb, healthy climate and its tranquillity. Paul Hogan, star of the two *Crocodile Dundee* movies, lives in the hinterland, and Olivia Newton-John, famous for her numerous international hits and starring role in the film musical *Grease*, also owns property in the area.

Above: *Kiama, a delightful seaside holiday-resort town south of Sydney, is famed for its blowhole. When the wind and waves are in the right direction, spumes of spray up to 20m (65ft) high are hurled out of a narrow fissure in the rocks.*

THE SNOWFIELDS

The New South Wales snowfields attract thousands of enthusiastic skiers from all over the world. Each winter the premier resorts of Thredbo village, Smiggin Holes, Perisher Valley, Blue Cow, Crackenback and Charlotte's Pass are filled to capacity with skiers who make the journey from the coast. Artificial snow-making equipment is available if the weather remains too warm. All the resorts have modern chalets and quality ski-lifts.

and wombats, lie close to the coast. However, beyond **Kiama** they fall back making way for the wide flood-plain of the Shoalhaven and the white sand beaches which edge **Jervis Bay**.

Jervis Bay is the home of one of the country's major naval training colleges. 7200ha (18 000 acres) of its southern headland was originally handed over to the Commonwealth on the novel grounds that Canberra and the ACT needed a sea port.

Edged by impressive national parks, the far south coast is a series of attractive villages where fishing, timber and dairy industries intermingle.

Eden, on the shores of Twofold Bay, was once a centre for whaling. **Narooma**, **Bermagui**, **Tathra** and **Ulladulla** all have thriving fishing fleets, and towns like **Kameruka**, **Bodalla** and **Bega** are synonymous with the cheeses commonly found on supermarket shelves.

If the north coast is about sun, surf and laziness, the south coast is more rural and more peaceful.

INLAND NEW SOUTH WALES

Beyond the coastal plains of New South Wales lie the magnificent tablelands of the Great Dividing Range. To the south, these tablelands form part of the **Snowy Mountains**, which is the highest mountain range in Australia. It is here that Australia's highest peak, **Mount Kosciuszko**, rises to 2228m (7310ft).

There was a time when the Snowy Mountains were a wilderness of steep ravines, narrow winding dirt roads and white snow gums. It was a superb, untamed region. Then, in 1949, the federal government established the Snowy Mountains Authority and over the next decade a hydro-electricity scheme was developed.

Thousands of workers from all over the world poured into the mountains to work on the vast project. The Snowy Mountains have always been an important subject of a romantic image of Australia. This is the place where the pioneers had to be tough, where the horse riders had to be the best, and where the conditions were most arduous in winter.

Once an area of wilderness and high-country sheep grazing, the mountains are now given over to tourism and electricity production. The old chalets have been replaced by modern, centrally heated hotels and in place of the dirt roads are a ski-tube railway system, high-speed ski-lifts and sealed highways.

For those eager to avoid the crowds, spring and summer are magical times in the mountains. When the skiers go and the snows melt away, the alpine flowers begin to bloom, the kangaroos and wombats reappear and, as the poet 'Banjo' Paterson observed, 'the air is clear as crystal, and the white stars fairly blaze'.

Spring and summer are times for bushwalking, visiting the beautiful **Yarrangobilly Caves**, swimming in the thermal pool, exploring the old gold diggings at **Kiandra**, and climbing to the top of Mount Kosciuszko.

Beyond the Great Dividing Range, New South Wales falls away into a series of low-lying slopes which eventually give way to the plains of the western region.

In turn, as the regular annual rainfall drops below 250mm (10in), these plains dwindle to a scrubby desert which is only good for vast sheep stations where hectares are needed to sustain a single sheep. It is a marginal wasteland where a car can drive along a straight road at 100kph (62mph) for two hours and see nothing other than the occasional kangaroo and endless plains of scrub and bush.

Towns like **Broken Hill** and **Silverton** have been used as bases for the making of several films like *A Town Like Alice, Wake in Fright, Mad Max, Razorback* and a dozen less successful productions. Beyond the film industry, the region is sustained by mining – at Broken Hill, White Cliffs and Silverton – and sheep.

Ports in the Desert

During the 19th century the Murray and Darling rivers were used extensively by paddle steamers to ship the rich wool clip to the coast. It is hard to imagine that inland towns like Wagga Wagga and Bourke were thriving ports. For decades Bourke was the transport centre for the whole of south-west Queensland and western NSW. At its height in the late 1800s over 40,000 bales of wool were being shipped down the Darling annually. The river transport continued until 1931.

Below: *The snowy slopes at Perisher Valley, Kosciuszko provide a playfield for the young and old.*

Above: *At Lightning Ridge, on the edge of the desert in far north-west New South Wales, miners dig for opals. They are, as one observer noted, 'monuments to the tenacious optimism of all mankind'. The work is hard but the rewards can be great.*

Highlights of Canberra

*** **New Parliament House** – excellent art displays and an opportunity to see Australian democracy in action.
** **Old Parliament House** – now a portrait gallery. A fascinating insight into Australian political life.
** **High Court** – a superb modern building. Guided tours are available.
** **Lake Burley Griffin** – walkways and bicycle ways around the lakes shores.
*** **Australian War Memorial** – a museum.

White Cliffs is a town which exists almost entirely underground. The local opal miners, in an attempt to avoid temperatures of over 40°C (104°F) in summer, have dug homes for themselves 10m (33ft) below the surface. There are underground dwellings in White Cliffs which would be considered mansions if they were above the surface. White Cliffs also has a solar energy source to supply the town with electricity.

From **Dubbo**, at the western edge of the central slopes, to **Broken Hill** the traveller drives for hours. The only stopping points on the Mitchell and Barrier highways are isolated townships (a combination of stop-off points for travellers and service centres for the surrounding property owners) such as Nyngan, Bourke, Cunnamulla, and Cobar. These forlorn little settlements put on a brave front to the outside world, but without the highways and the sheep stations they would have no reason to exist.

Canberra and the Australian Capital Territory (ACT)

Canberra is an artificial city created as a result of the federation of Australian states. In 1908, 2330 sq km (900 sq miles) of good quality sheep-grazing land was carved out of New South Wales, and on 1 January 1911, the Australian Capital Territory was handed over officially to the commonwealth government.

That same year, a competition was launched for the design of a city for 25,000 people. The competition was won by an American, Walter Burley Griffin, whose design based on a series of geometrically precise circles and axes, was similar to the street patterns of Washington and Paris.

Today, Canberra is a city of great beauty, with broad roadways, superb parklands, and many elegant buildings. On a clear spring or autumn day it is a city which is captivating in its graciousness.

The visitor arriving in Canberra is treated with the kind of attention one would expect from bureaucrats. The information is excellent and it is easy to spend a couple of days visiting the **National Art Gallery** (which now boasts

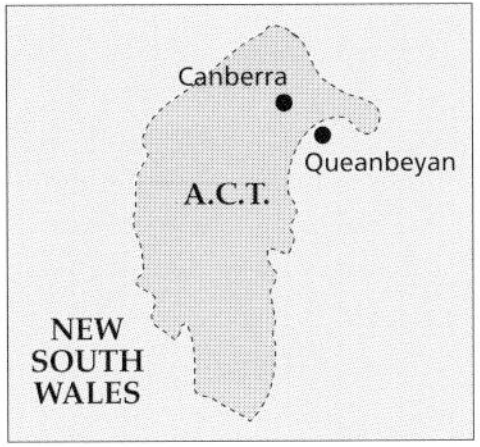

Left: *Canberra's Lake Burley Griffin is a magnet for visitors. There are walks around the lake's edge, boats and bicycles for hire, views across the lake and, most days, the spectacular sight of the Captain Cook Memorial Water Jet shooting water up to 140m (460ft) into the air.*

a superb collection of works), the **National Library**, the **Australian War Memorial**, the old and new **Parliament Houses**, the **Film and Sound Archive** (which shows early Australian movies) and the **High Court.**

For people who want simpler pleasures there are boats for hire and a pleasant row or cruise around Lake Burley Griffin offers a very different view of the city.

FLORIADE

Canberra is breathtakingly beautiful in both spring and autumn. The decision to plant the city with deciduous European trees and extensive flower beds has meant that the displays of new blooms and changing colours are spectacular. **Floriade**, held every spring (usually October), displays more than half a million flowers and features a fortnight of interesting events.

Sydney and New South Wales at a Glance

Best Times To Visit

September to **November** (spring) Sydney comes alive with parks and gardens full of the city's famous azalea and rhododendron displays.
December to **February** (summer) the city, which is abundantly supplied with beaches, certainly knows how to take full advantage of the long, hot summer days.

Getting There

Sydney (Kingsford Smith) **Airport** has both international and domestic terminals. They are 5km (3 miles) away from each other and 9km (6 miles) from the city centre.
Airport Express Buses, coloured green and gold, operate every 10 minutes from both terminals to well-mapped routes in the city and Kings Cross with stops at most of the major hotels. There is also the **Kingsford Smith Airport Bus** service which operates half hourly and will usually do specified drop-offs and pick-ups; tel: (02) 9667-3221. Ring the day before for pick-up service.

Taxis are plentiful and will take you anywhere. Major car rental firms are represented at the airport.

Interstate bus services to and from Sydney are frequent and efficient. Remember distances are vast and bus travel can be time consuming – e.g. Sydney to Melbourne takes 13 hours. **Bus Australia**, tel: (02) 9261-1888.
Greyhound/Pioneer, tel: (02) 9286-8600.

There is an extensive railway system in NSW called **Countrylink**. Interstate travel can also be booked, tel: 132232.

Getting Around

There are three types of public transport in Sydney: buses, trains and ferries. All are clearly marked and signposted. For information on these forms of transport ring **Buses, Trains and Ferries**, tel: 131500.

Timetables for the three services can be picked up at the information booth at Circular Quay. The **Explorer**, a tourist bus which operates a continuous loop around the tourist sightsy, runs every 20 minutes. The stops are marked by green and red signs.

The suburban trains are fast and efficient, they are clearly marked and colour coded. The ferry system is the nicest way to get around this harbour city. For instance the Taronga Zoo Ferry takes visitors from Circular Quay to the zoo in 12 minutes.

Car rental firms are prolific and competitive and are advertised everywhere.

Where to Stay

Sydney is well serviced by hotels, motels and serviced apartments. The central business district has a large range of accommodation, but don't forget the quieter suburban areas. Public transport makes the city centre easy to get to.
Hyde Park Plaza Hotel, College St, luxury apartments located in the city centre with excellent facilities, tel: (02) 9331-6933, fax: 9331-6022.
Hotel Inter-Continental, Macquarie St, a luxury hotel partly housed in the historic treasury building (1851) in the centre of the city, tel: (02) 9230-0200, fax: 9240-1240.
Parkroyal Darling Harbour, Day St, opposite the famous Darling Harbour complex, a quality hotel with excellent service, tel: (02) 9261-4444, fax 9261-8766.
Sydney Regent Hotel, George St, the best views in Sydney from this luxury hotel, tel: (02) 9238-8000, fax: 9251-2851.

Budget Accommodation

Harbour Rocks Hotel, Harrington St, medium-sized hotel in the heart of the Rocks area, the oldest section of Sydney, tel: (02) 9251-8944, fax: 9251-8900.
The Cambridge, Riley St, well-located, reasonably priced hotel with all the facilities, tel: (02) 9212-2111, fax: 9281-1981.
Kendall Hotel, Potts Point, Victorian-style guest house situated in a leafy quiet suburb, tel: (02) 9357-3200, fax: 9357-7606.

Sydney and New South Wales at a Glance

Where to Eat

Every conceivable variety of food is on offer in this cosmopolitan city. Restaurants cluster in pockets. **Oxford St** from Hyde Park through Darlinghurst ending at Paddington has a large selection. **Glebe Point Rd** in Glebe offers over 40 restaurants. Another good area is **King St** in Newtown. There are several magazines that cover restaurants. *This Week in Sydney* is put out by the NSW Government Tourist Travel Centre. Widely recognised as authoritative is the *Sydney Morning Herald*'s, *Good Food Guide,* available in newsagencies throughout the city.

Bayswater Brasserie, Kings Cross, stylish brasserie with excellent service, tel: (02) 9357-2177.

Doyles on the Beach, Watsons Bay, seafood restaurant on the beach overlooking the harbour, tel: (02) 9337-2077.

Harbour Restaurant, Sydney Opera House, dine in style at one of Sydney's most famous landmarks, tel: (02) 9250-7191.

Imperial Peking Harbourside Restaurant, Circular Quay West, Sydney's most famous Chinese restaurant opposite the Opera House, tel: (02) 9247-7073.

John Cadman, No. 6 Jetty, Circular Quay, cruise the harbour while you enjoy excellent cuisine, tel: (02) 9206-6666.

Jordan's Seafood Restaurant, Darling Harbour, good seafood served in the fun atmosphere of Darling Harbour, tel: (02) 9281-3711.

Tours and Excursions

AAT Kings has an extensive range of one- and two-day tours. A popular excursion is to Canberra, tel: (02) 9252-2788.

Australian Pacific Tours offers a wide range of coach tours fanning out from Sydney. Their most popular is the daily tour to the Blue Mountains, tel: (02) 9247-7222, fax 9247-2052.

Clipper Gray Line has a wide range of coach tours to most areas around Sydney, tel: (02) 9241-3983.

Matilda Harbour Cruises depart four times a day from Darling Harbour, and the luncheon cruise offers a steak and seafood BBQ, tel: (02) 9264-7377, fax: 9290-3858.

Captain Cook Cruises offers a wonderful look at the Sydney Harbour, your ticket is valid all day so you can feel free to get off and explore, departs from Circular Quay, tel: (02) 9206-1111, fax: 9206-1179.

Sydney Harbour Seaplanes offer a view of the harbour that is unique. Take off and land in the harbour, tel: (02) 9918-7472, fax: 9371-0047.

See Sydney from the back of a Harley Davidson with **Eastcoast Motorcycle Tours.** Also travel further afield to the Northern Beaches and Blue Mountains, tel: (02) 9544-2400.

The New South Wales Travel Centre, York St, has a large range of tour and excursion brochures and helpful information, they can make bookings for you, tel: 132077, fax: (02) 9224-4411.

Useful Contacts

Sydney Visitors Information Centre, Martin Place – this conveniently located information booth can answer most of your questions about Sydney. It has a large assortment of pamphlets and brochures and will answer phone enquiries between 09:00 and 17:00. tel: (02) 9235-2424.

SYDNEY	J	F	M	A	M	J	J	A	S	O	N	D
AVERAGE TEMP. °F	73	73	72	66	63	57	54	57	61	64	68	72
AVERAGE TEMP. °C	23	23	22	19	17	14	12	14	16	18	20	22
Hours of Sun Daily	8	7	7	6	6	6	7	8	8	8	8	8
SEA TEMP. °F	73	75	75	73	70	68	66	63	63	68	68	72
SEA TEMP. °C	23	24	24	23	21	20	19	17	17	20	20	22
RAINFALL in	4	4.5	5.3	5	4.8	5.1	3.9	3.2	2.7	3.1	3.2	3
RAINFALL mm	104	117	135	129	121	131	100	81	69	79	82	78
Days of Rainfall	12	12	13	12	12	12	10	10	10	11	11	12

3
Brisbane and Queensland

Queensland is Australia's second-largest state. In spite of its vast size, most of the state is marginal land moving towards desert. If it isn't desert it's impenetrable rainforest or swampy, mangrove wetlands. Consequently, the majority of the state's three million people live in Brisbane or along the coast in large urban sprawls like the **Gold Coast**, the **Sunshine Coast**, and the major cities of **Townsville**, **Bundaberg**, **Cairns** and **Rockhampton**.

The state is cut in half by the Tropic of Capricorn. It is also divided by the Great Dividing Range which starts about 200km (125 miles) south of Cape York, and runs in a series of low-lying ranges and tablelands down the eastern coastline.

Historically, the coast has been one of the state's main agricultural regions. The waters are rich with fish and crustaceans. The slopes of the Great Dividing Range were an important source of valuable tropical timber and the alluvial coastal plains have been ideal for tropical crops such as sugar-cane, pineapples, mangoes, bananas, and pawpaws.

In recent times, agriculture has declined in importance. The great boom industry is tourism. Over 60% of all tourists arriving in Australia nominate Queensland as their primary destination. In 1994, it had over 60 international hotels and tourist resorts, more than a dozen huge marinas, and a network of ancillary facilities such as casinos, charter cruises, sporting complexes, and hundreds of motels and restaurants.

Don't Miss

*** **Botanic Gardens** showcasing superb tropical plants beside the Brisbane River.
** **Queensland Cultural Centre** including the museum and library.
** **Moreton Bay** and **Stradbroke Island** are well worth a leisurely cruise.
* **Government House**.

Opposite: *Fraser Island, the largest sand island in the world, is one of the wonders of Queensland. Its quiet, unspoilt beauty symbolises the special charm of much of the Queensland coast.*

Opposite top:
Brisbane is an attractive, modern city where high-rise buildings are mirrored in the quietly flowing waters of the Brisbane River. The city's air of informality makes it different from all the other state capitals.

Brisbane

In his book, *Portrait of Brisbane,* Bill Scott wrote: 'Brisbane is a lazy town with its sleeves rolled up, casually sprawling across its thirty-seven hills.'

This image of a subtropical city which thrives on informality still captures the spirit of the city today.

Brisbane is no ordinary state capital. Queensland, because of its size and its decentralisation, can claim Brisbane as its centre of government while still acknowledging the regional importance of cities like **Townsville** and **Rockhampton.**

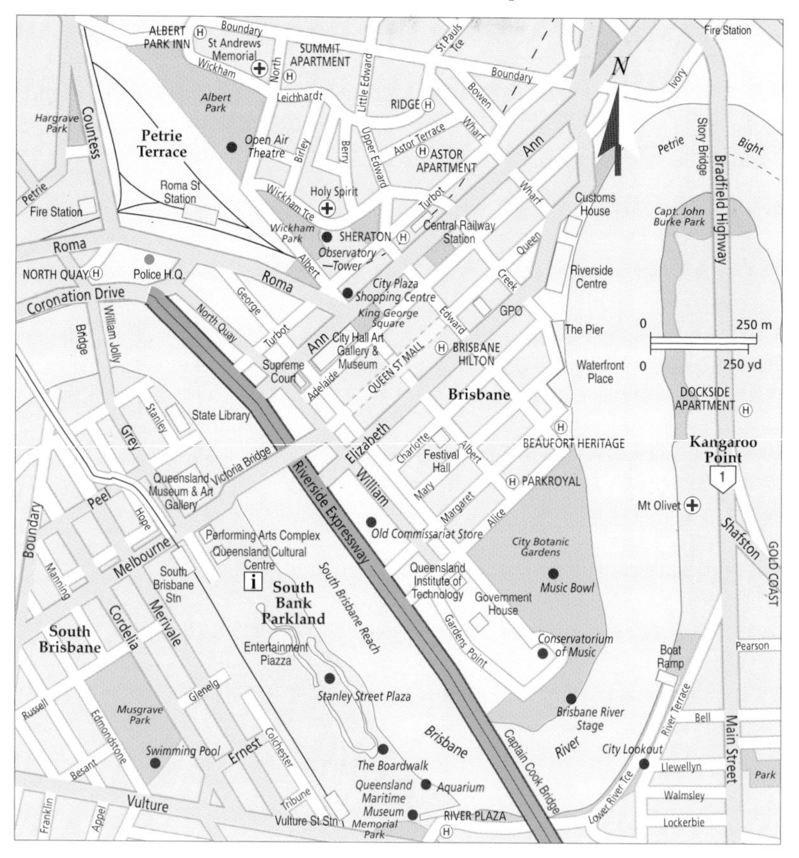

City Sightseeing

Brisbane has long had a tradition of newness and, as a result, it has relatively few genuinely old public buildings of importance. However, the remaining old buildings are gracious and impressive.

The most interesting landmarks in the city include **The Old Windmill**, sometimes known as **Observatory Tower**, and the **The Old Commissariat Store** at 111 William Street which was built by convicts when Brisbane was a closed penal colony. It is now the headquarters of the Royal Historical Society of Queensland.

Another significant landmark is the **City Hall Art Gallery** and **Museum** complex, which combines **King George Square**, the **Brisbane Administration Centre** and the **City Plaza Shopping Centre**. The clock tower, which rises 91m (300ft) above the City Plaza, provides excellent panoramic views of the city.

Climate

Brisbane's climate is subtropical with an average annual rainfall of 1090mm (43in), most of which falls between December and March, an average of over seven hours of sunshine each day, a humidity level which hovers around 50% for all the year, and a temperature range from 10°C (50°F) in winter to 30°C (86°F) in summer.

City of Tropical Parks

Brisbane's warm, moist climate ensures that the city's 200 parks and gardens are its greatest attraction. Be sure to see the dome-shaped indoor display at Mount Coot-tha which houses a virtual tropical rainforest and the displays of orchids, flame trees, bougainvilleas, frangipanis, oleanders and jacarandas, which make the City Botanic Gardens so impressive. The park at South Bank offers excellent views of the city.

Left: *Brisbane's South Bank complex offers a cultural centre, a performing arts centre and a swimming pool, which is more in keeping with a faraway tropical island than the centre of a modern city.*

MOUNT COOT-THA BOTANIC GARDENS AND RESERVE

Located off Mount Coot-tha Road in Toowong, only 10 minutes from the city centre, the Mount Coot-tha Gardens are reputed to be Australia's largest subtropical display of flora. They cover an area of 57ha (140 acres) in which plants are set against an environment of lakes, ponds and streams. The indoor displays ensure that even in winter the gardens are worth a visit.

Located just over the Victoria Bridge from the city's central business district is **South Bank**. This includes the **John Oxley Library**, the **Queensland Museum** with its two million items, including the tiny 'Avian Cirrus' aeroplane in which Bert Hinkler made the first solo flight from England to Australia in 1928, and the **Performing Arts Complex** with its Lyric Theatre, Concert Hall and Cremorne Studio Theatre.

At 261 Queen Street, the **General Post Office** is located on the site of the city's original female convict barracks. On the first floor is the GPO Museum which exhibits a range of old postal, radio and telegraphic equipment.

Located between the **Queensland Institute of Technology** and the **Brisbane River** is the **old Government House,** which was built in 1862. It is currently used as the offices for the National Trust of Queensland.

The **Queensland Maritime Museum** is situated on the river at the end of Dock Street. The museum features an interesting display of charts, model ships, engines and memorabilia, combined with 'on the water' displays of a World War II frigate and an old steam tug.

In Petrie Terrace, the old **Victoria Barracks** were built between 1864 and 1874 to a design which had been drawn up by the War Office in London. Today, the barracks are a military museum housing weapons, old uniforms, photographs and memorabilia.

GOLD COAST BEACHES

There are nine major beaches along the Gold Coast. Each is excellent for sunbathing, swimming and surfing.

- Coolangatta – fun for the whole family.
- Currumbin – more famous for its bird sanctuary than its beach.
- Palm Beach.
- Burleigh Heads.
- Nobby Beach.
- Mermaid Beach.
- Broadbeach – in the heart of the tourist action.
- Surfers Paradise – the most famous of all the beaches. A long sandy strip backed by high-rise apartments.
- Southport – the more modern and exclusive end of the coast.

Parks and Gardens

Brisbane has nearly 200 parks and reserves within the city. The City Botanic Gardens cover over 20ha (50 acres) of land. Beautifully located on the banks of the Brisbane River and spreading over the gentle slopes and undulations below Parliament House and the old Government House, the gardens are a peaceful respite from the bustle of the central business district.

Opposite: *Surfers Paradise is one of Australia's premier holiday destinations. High-rise holiday apartments and hotels offer thousands of rooms overlooking the long sunny stretch of beach. Casinos, nightclubs and restaurants abound in the area.*

The Gold Coast

The Gold Coast is Australia's most famous tourist area. Since the 1950s, it has developed to house innumerable motels and hotels, eateries, a casino and several high-profile attractions including **Warner Bros. Movie World** and **Sea World.**

The high-rise development which has occurred along the coast has not met with universal approval. Still, the area continues to act as a magnet. Its population doubles every decade. It attracts thousands of holiday-makers during the summer months, and its New Year's Eve Party and end-of-school celebrations have become legendary.

In the hinterland behind the Gold Coast there are stretches of unspoilt rainforest, spectacular waterfalls and the beautifully rugged Lamington National Park. The peacefulness of the villages and the quietness of the shops stands in sharp contrast to the exuberance of the coast.

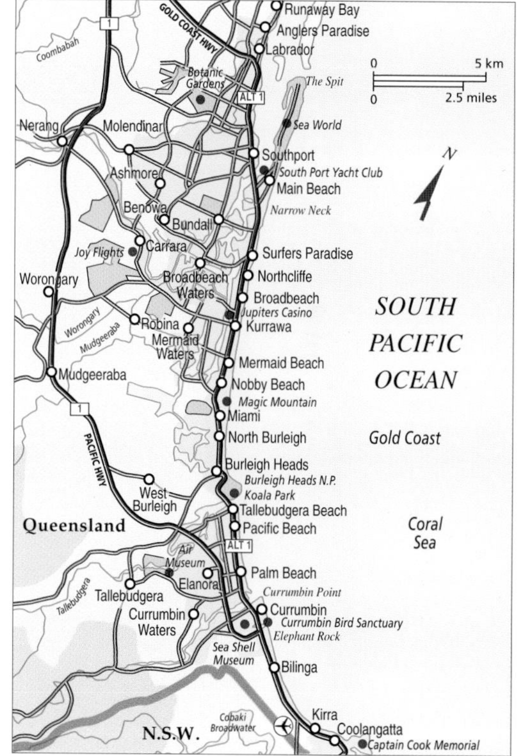

Gold Coast Holiday Attractions

There's the multi-million dollar **Conrad International Hotel** complex which includes **Jupiters Casino** where popular Japanese gambling games like Keno and Sic-Bo vie with Baccarat, Roulette, Blackjack and the all-Australian Two-up. There's **Sanctuary Cove** and the low-rise luxury of the **Sheraton Mirage Gold Coast** with its marina and lagoon. The **Wet'n'Wild Cades County** has the only man-made pool in Australia with one-metre waves and life-guards, and the exclusive Sanctuary Cove boasts an 18-hole golf course designed by Arnold Palmer.

The Sunshine Coast

Travelling north from Brisbane, the visitor must first pass through the **Sunshine Coast** to beautiful **Fraser Island** (the largest sand island in the world), through the beef and cattle country between **Gladstone** and **Mackay**, and the densely-covered tropical rainforest areas which stretch from **Townsville** to **Cape York**.

Nothing captures the spirit of the Sunshine Coast quite like the **Big Pineapple**, a theme park based on pineapple production. To indicate its entrance, a huge replica of a pineapple sits, golden and gleaming, beside the Bruce Highway, just south of **Nambour**. 'Take a genuine Sugar Cane Train ride, hop aboard the fun Nutmobile. Little ones will love petting the kangaroos,' declares the advertisement.

Lying north of Brisbane, the Sunshine Coast has developed rapidly as a major attraction for tourists. Its advantages are largely connected to a more up-market appeal. A thriving centre like **Noosa**, now the home of tennis champion Evonne Cawley, is far more sophisticated than any part of the Gold Coast.

Historically, this was a typical tropical rural area. In recent times, the agricultural base has expanded to include ginger, macadamia nuts and lesser-known tropical fruits.

Right: *First sighted and named by Captain Cook, the Glasshouse Mountains, 61km (38 miles) north of Brisbane, are a series of volcanic plugs (the surrounding material has been slowly eroded away) of rhyolite and trachyte which are estimated to be between 24 and 25 million years old.*
Opposite: *The Great Barrier Reef is one of the wonders of the world. There is no better way to experience its beauty than to sail to the outer reef and explore the wonderland of fish and coral formations.*

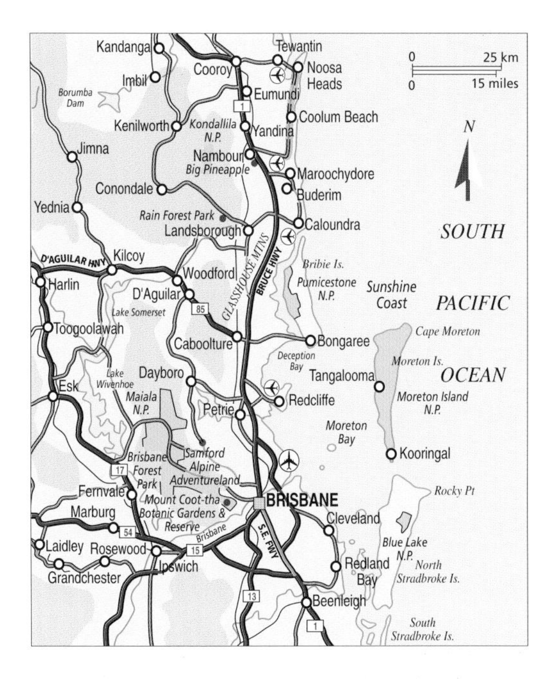

Facts About the Great Barrier Reef

- In 1975 the Great Barrier Reef Marine Park Authority was established. The Reef was placed on the World Heritage List in 1981.
- All the holiday islands offer trips to the Reef.
- The stony corals which produce reefs grow best between 22 and 28°C (72 and 82°F), they need lots of sunlight – below 60m (200ft) there is insufficient light – and they prosper where there is little muddying of the waters by rivers or, more recently, human pollution.

Away from the coast, in the area around the spectacular extinct volcanoes of the **Glasshouse Mountains**, for example, dairy farming is still the dominant industry.

The area is currently committed to over A$1 billion worth of tourist development and the popularity of the major centres is such that demand for accommodation is increasing at the rate of 22% per year.

The Great Barrier Reef

The Great Barrier Reef is made up of more than 2100 separate reefs and covers over 230 000km^2 (88,780 sq miles). It is the largest structure built by living creatures.

The cliché 'underwater wonderland' is a remarkably apt description of the Reef. Its formations, from the huge red sea fans to the luxuriant coral cays, are breathtaking and its fish, crustaceans, anemones and sea wasps (more commonly known as box jellyfish) are mysterious, beautiful and exotic.

Fraser Island

Fraser Island ranks as one of the true wonders of Australia. It is the largest sand island in the world and has such a range of attractions and activities that it is a 'must' for anyone travelling along the Queensland coast. It is on Fraser Island that the visitor can see extraordinary freshwater sand dune lakes, beautiful quiet streams, cliffs with remarkable coloured sand horizons, and rugged headlands.

The economy of the Reef is based on tourism. There are 24 island resorts, including the coral cays of Heron, Green and Fraser islands and the resorts of Magnetic Island near Townsville, Hayman Island, Hamilton Island, Dunk Island and the Whitsunday group (which includes South Molle, Daydream, Brampton and Lindeman islands). From the mainland the most popular centres for exploring the Reef are at Townsville and Cairns.

Cairns

Cairns is a boom town. Tourism has seen it change from a quiet port to an international resort. It is an ideal access point to the Great Barrier Reef and the train journey to the tiny township of Kuranda offers the visitor a unique opportunity to experience the local Aboriginal culture in the **Tjapukai Dance Theatre**.

Behind Cairns lie the lush and unspoiled **Atherton Tablelands** where maize, beef and dairy cattle, peanuts, timber and potatoes are regarded as the cornerstones of the local economy.

Kuranda's Aboriginal Theatre

The Tjapukai Theatre makes a visit to Kuranda worthwhile. This truly remarkable group have managed to create a show which is a mixture of the educational, the entertaining, and the emotionally rewarding. It is a powerful statement of what it means to be an Aborigine.

The power of the show rests on its mixture; each dancer explains a particular aspect of Aboriginal life ranging from the boomerang to the didgeridoo, songsticks, spears and clothing, a clever blend of ancient and modern, the enactment of a tribal legend, a buoyant sense of humour, and a constantly reiterated theme of 'Proud to be an Aborigine'.

THE FAR NORTH

To the west and north of Cairns lies the Far North of Queensland – a region characterised by tropical rainforest along the coast, dry inland areas, and one of the richest concentrations of flora and fauna anywhere in Australia. This is an area of vast distances, few towns – **Mossman**, **Port Douglas**, **Weipa**, **Cooktown** – and a few tiny settlements like **Bamaga** at the tip of the **Cape York Peninsula**. The rough dirt roads are often cut by creeks and rivers.

The road from Cairns to Bamaga is over 900km (560 miles) long. The local Aborigines live on outlying reserves and the only industry of any importance began in 1955, when Weipa was confirmed as the site of the largest bauxite deposit in the world.

Because of the poor roads and inhospitable terrain, much of Cape York has remained untouched, but there are some wonderful national parks that are worth the hike. Only the area between Cairns and Cooktown has been subject to any kind of commercial and agricultural development. In this area, tropical fruit is grown, tea plantations have been established, and both commercial and game fishing are practised.

There has been controversy about the development of the **Daintree** for tourism, but it is a marvellous experience to cross the Daintree and move through the tropical rainforest to Cape Tribulation with its mangrove coastline.

Opposite: *The Aboriginal dancers in the Tjapukai Theatre are dedicated to the preservation and portrayal of Aboriginal dance.*

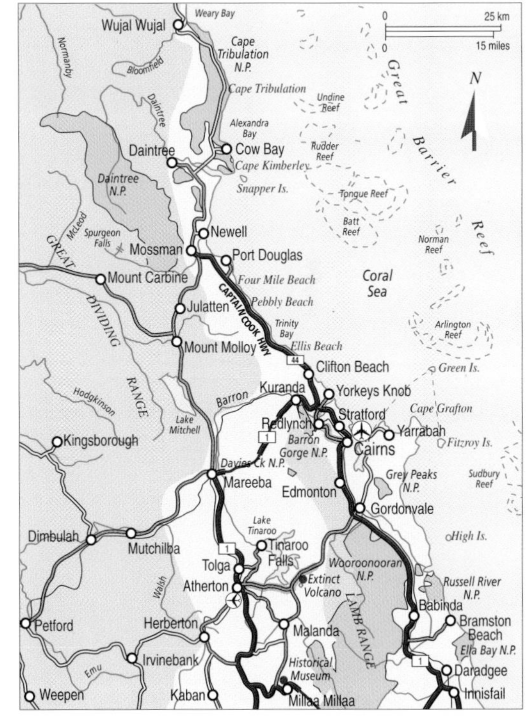

Right: *Port Douglas, north of Cairns, is one of Queensland's most luxurious resort towns. Once a wild gold-mining port, it is now noted for its chic shopping facilities and Barrier Reef cruises. This large anchor is part of Ben Cropp's Shipwreck Museum which is located at the end of the wharf.*
Opposite: *The marker a few kilometres from the Combo Waterhole reminds visitors of its link to Australian history.*

Gulf Country

The Gulf Country is bounded by the Great Dividing Range and the Atherton Tablelands to the east, the Northern Territory to the west, and the Gulf of Carpentaria to the north.

This is a wilderness of mangrove swamps with a summer monsoon season when temperatures climb over 40°C (over 104°F), the humidity is unbearable and the heavy monsoonal rains fall with monotonous regularity.

But the Gulf is more than a dangerous wilderness. **Karumba**, the sole port of the Gulf, is home to both a prawning fleet and Queensland's lucrative barramundi industry. Croydon was once the centre of an important gold-mining industry and gems like topaz, garnet and aquamarine can still be found in the eastern savannah.

The real interest of the Gulf lies in the antiquity of its Aboriginal culture (it is known that Aborigines have lived there continuously for the last 35,000 years) and the extraordinary richness of its wildlife.

The Gulf Country

The Gulf is part of the true outback. Narrow roads and tiny towns are typical. Add to this the harsh notice: *'WARNING – Please remember at all times that the prehistoric crocodile lives in the river systems of the Gulf Savannah and it is important to believe the local words of warning:* "Whatever you put in the water be prepared to lose it". *Crocodiles are a reality and Gulf rivers are their natural habitat. Because you can't see them most definitely does not mean they are not there.'*

Beyond the Coast

Queensland is a vast flat area which slowly moves from savannah grassland to desert beyond the coast. The towns are isolated, the accommodation is basic and often the water supply comes from artesian bores, bubbling up from hundreds of metres below the surface.

The whole area is marginal agricultural land and it ceases to be even marginal when the edge of the **Simpson Desert National Park** is reached some 100km (62 miles) to the west of Birdsville. Life here can be hard and the people justifiably regard their lonely existence with considerable pride.

Throughout the inland there are places which mean a lot to Australians. The **Combo Waterhole** near **Kynuna** is said to be the billabong into which 'Banjo' Paterson's jolly swagman jumped. The tiny town of **McKinley** was renamed 'Walkabout Creek' for Paul Hogan's *Crocodile Dundee*. **Mount Isa** is the world's largest single producer of lead and zinc and the largest city in the world (in area) covering a total of 41,255km^2 (16,000 sq miles).

The inland is also noted for its rich diversity of wildlife. Brolgas, flocks of black and white cockatoos, wild pigs, corellas, kangaroos and emus abound. If the rains of the monsoonal wet season reach the headwaters of the dusty **Diamantina** and **Cooper Creek** rivers, large areas of the south-west can be converted into a vast lake.

This is still frontier land. It is harsh and inhospitable with roads suitable for four-wheel-drive vehicles only.

STOCKMAN'S HALL OF FAME

The A$12.5-million 'Australian Stockman's Hall of Fame' at Longreach is the premier destination in central Queensland. It should be called 'The Australian History Timeline'. Its exhibitions include a model of Aboriginal cave paintings, the First Fleet, the early settlement in Sydney, the major explorations, the early pioneers (with a model slab hut, a hawker's van and a blacksmith's shop), the pastoral expansion, and then a focus on life in the bush up to the present day.

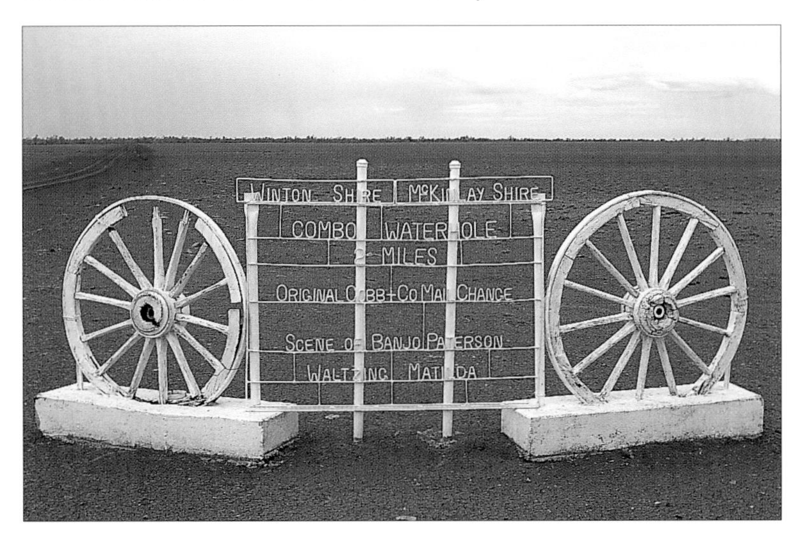

Brisbane and Queensland at a Glance

Best Times To Visit

Queensland's seasons are divided into a 'wet' and a 'dry'. During the 'wet', rain and cyclones hit the coast. This occurs through the summer months. The best time to visit is from **June** to **September** (dry). This is officially winter, however, the days are warm and balmy and the nights cool and pleasant.

Getting There

The Brisbane **international** and **domestic airports** are close to each other and are about 12km (8 miles) north-east of the city centre. **Coachtrans** runs a shuttle bus from both terminals to the Transit Centre in the city every half hour from 05:00 to 23:00. **Taxis** are available at both airports as are the major **car rental** firms. The **Transit Centre** in Roma St is the main terminus and booking point for all long-distance trains and buses. Brisbane is well serviced by both. The XPT train from Sydney takes 14 hours and runs daily. The major bus companies all travel to and from the capital cities to Brisbane.

Getting Around

The bus service in Brisbane is efficient and easy to use. Bus-stops in the city centre are colour coded for convenience. The **city circle bus** does a clockwise loop every five minutes. The **Citytrain** network has seven lines running to the suburbs. All trains go through the Transit Centre in Roma St. Car rental firms are well represented. All the larger major companies operate and there are also many smaller rental agencies. The **Brisbane River** is an active waterway, particularly for visitors. It flows through the centre of the city. There are a number of ferry and cruise ships offering interesting journeys along the river.

Where to Stay

Brisbane is both a tourist destination and the capital of Queensland. As such it has a thriving city centre and a wide range of accommodation. The city offers everything from luxury five star, serviced apartments to bed and breakfast.

Beaufort Heritage, Cnr Margaret & Edwards sts, centrally located, luxurious hotel near the waterside and Botanic Gardens, tel: (07) 3221-1999, fax: 3221-6895.

Brisbane Hilton, Elizabeth St, The Hilton's usual excellent service and style is evident everywhere in this hotel, tel: (07) 3231-3131, fax: 3231-3199.

All Seasons Abbey Plaza Hotel, Roma St, centrally located quality accommodation with excellent facilities, tel: (07) 3236-1444, fax: 3236-1134.

North Quay Hotel, North Quay, hotel in the heart of the city overlooking the Brisbane River, some suites with cooking facilities, tel: (07) 3236-1440, fax: 3236-4159.

Budget Accommodation

Bellevue Hotel, George St, centrally located, well-priced hotel, with all the facilities of a more expensive hotel, tel: (07) 3221-6044, fax: 3221-7474.

Brisbane City Travelodge, Roma St, good clean accommodation with excellent facilities, well located, tel: (07) 3238-2222, fax: 3238-2288.

Gateway Hotel, North Quay, overlooks the Brisbane River and South Bank parklands, central location, tel: (07) 3236 3300, fax: 3236-1035.

Marrs Town House, Wickham Ter, value accommodation from inexpensive rooms to luxury apartments, tel: (07) 3831-5388, fax: 3839-0060.

Where to Eat

Brisbane has a large and varied selection of restaurants catering to all tastes.

Queensland is famous for its seafood: mud crab, Moreton Bay bugs and barramundi. Tender beef and wonderful fruits do not take a back seat. Check *This Week in Brisbane* put out by **The Queensland Government Travel Centre**, also *Dining*

Brisbane and Queensland at a Glance

Out, a magazine sponsored by the Brisbane Visitors and Convention Bureau.
Coronation Seafood, Coronation Dve, exceptional seafood restaurant where only the freshest fish is served, tel: (07) 3369-9955.
Jean Pierre's, Boundary St, excellent cuisine beautifully served at a reasonable price, tel: (07) 3839-9831.
Michael's Riverside Restaurant, Riverside Centre, river views give this restaurant a special appeal, Italian and traditional cuisine are served in two dining rooms, tel: (07) 3832-5522.
Mount Coot-tha Summit Restaurant, Mount Coot-tha, an incredible view over the city and out to Moreton Bay at this mountain-top restaurant, tel: (07) 3369-9922.
Pier Nine, cnr Mary & Eagle sts, fresh fish cooked with flair, lovely river views, tel: (07) 3229-2194.
Siggi's at the Heritage, cnr Edward & Margaret Sts, part of the Heritage Hotel, elegant old-world charm, European cooking at its best, tel: (07) 3221-4555.

Tours and Excursions

Brisbane Paddlewheeler departs from No. 1 Pier North Quay. This old world paddle-wheeler cruises the Brisbane river both day and night, tel: (07) 3846-1713.
Boomerang Tours departs from the Travel Centre, has a wide variety of coach tours, tel: (07) 3211-2484.
Discover Brisbane bus tour run by the city council makes 20 stops of interest around the city. Takes in most major sites, tel: (07) 3225-4444.
Riverside Ferry Company departs from Redland Bay and travels to North Stradbroke Island five times daily, tel: (07) 3358-2122.
A1 Tours travel through the Lamington National Park, wildlife and subtropical rainforest are a feature, tel: (07) 3268-6329.
Great Barrier Reef Tours fly to beautiful Lady Musgrave Island on the Coral Lagoon tour and explore the beautiful tropical lagoon, tel: (07) 3268-6329.
Save the Koala Tours run a tour to the Lone Pine Koala Sanctuary. This is Australia's best known animal sanctuary, tel: (07) 3229-7233.
St Helena's Guided Tours visit historic St Helena Island, an early penal colony, they also offer charter trips, tel: (07) 3262-7422.
Sunshine Balloons early morning hot-air ballooning over Brisbane city, Beenleigh and Gatton, wonderful way to see the beauty of Queensland. Champagne breakfast on landing, flights daily, tel: (07) 3208-6527.

Useful Contacts

Royal Automobile Club of Queensland, Edward St, offers a comprehensive series of road maps and helpful information for the traveller, tel: (07) 3361-2444.
Queensland National Parks & Wildlife Service, a must for explorers and bush walkers located on Ann St, open Monday to Friday during business hours.
The Great South East Tourist Association is conveniently located at the Transit Centre, can provide information on Brisbane and the surrounding areas, tel: (07) 3236 2020.
The Queensland Government Travel Centre on the corner of Adelaide and Edward sts, is primarily a booking office for tours and excursions, tel: (07) 3221 6111.

BRISBANE	J	F	M	A	M	J	J	A	S	O	N	D
AVERAGE TEMP. °F	77	77	75	72	66	63	61	64	68	72	75	77
AVERAGE TEMP. °C	25	25	24	22	19	17	16	18	20	22	24	25
Hours of Sun Daily	8	7	7	7	7	7	7	8	8	8	8	8
SEA TEMP. °F	77	77	77	77	73	72	68	66	66	66	72	73
SEA TEMP. °C	25	25	25	25	23	22	20	19	19	19	22	23
RAINFALL in	6.3	6.2	5.5	3.7	2.9	2.7	2.2	1.9	1.8	3	3.8	5.3
RAINFALL mm	160	158	141	94	74	68	57	47	46	76	97	134
Days of Rainfall	13	13	15	11	10	8	7	7	7	5	10	12

4 Melbourne and Victoria

Covering 227,620km² (87,900 sq miles), only 3% of mainland Australia, Victoria is the smallest of all the mainland states.

Melbourne has been, for significant periods in Australia's history, the country's unofficial capital city. In 1888, the year of the country's centennial celebrations, Melbourne was the most populous city in Australia, and it was the seat of Federal Government until the Parliament House was built in Canberra.

Victoria, or the Port Phillip District as it was known, remained part of New South Wales until 1851. It was settled in 1803 by **Lieutenant David Collins** who, with a small group of convicts and free settlers, established a camp at Port Phillip Bay.

Collins was followed by **John Batman**, who, in June 1835, signed a treaty with the local Aborigines and 'purchased' 243,000ha (600,000 acres) from them.

Today, Victoria is a state rich in resources, with a strong and productive economic base. Despite its size it is home to over 25% of Australia's population.

Primarily a fine wool and fat lamb producer, it is also a beef, wheat and dairy producer, with nearly three million beef cattle and 1.5 million dairy cattle in the state.

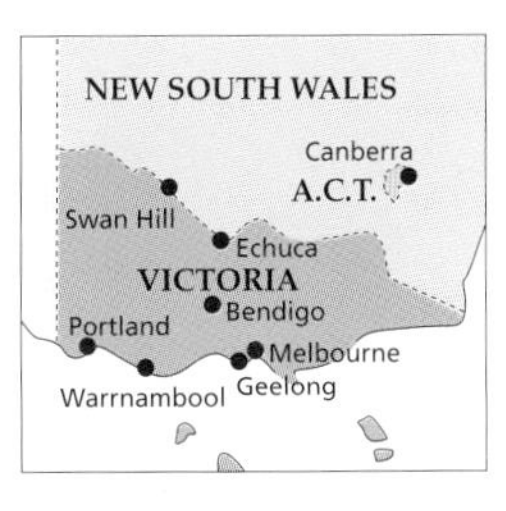

Don't Miss

*** **National Gallery of Victoria:** one of the finest in Australia with excellent exhibitions and permanent displays of works by Australia's best artists.
** **The Yarra River:** may be muddy but walks along the banks and cruises are well worth the stroll.
** **Captain Cook's Cottage:** in the Fitzroy Gardens, was brought out to Australia from England.
** **Tram:** Travelling around the inner city is a must.

Melbourne

Melbourne is the capital of Victoria. It is a sophisticated and cultured modern city and is now recognised as the second-largest city in Australia with a population of 3,187,500 in 1993.

Opposite: *The parks which run along both sides of the Yarra River are ideal for walking, picnics and barbeques.*

Climate

Melbourne has a mean average temperature of 15°C (59°F) and an annual rainfall of 657mm (26in) which rises to 889mm (35in) in the ranges to the west of the city.

The city has a reputation for unreliable weather. Even locals will admit that the weather can provide four seasons in one day.

It is a city suffering from urban sprawl. Ribbons of urban development spread out into the commuter belts of the Dandenong Range and the beachside suburbs.

Gold gave the city its greatest boost. It saw the establishment of roads, railway lines and a substantial water reservoir. As the population of the city grew, so the demands upon the surrounding agricultural lands became tailored to the needs of the local community. Dairy farms provided the city with milk. Crops of domestic vegetables were grown on the plains, while orchards were planted in the nearby mountains.

It is very easy for first-time visitors to find their way around the centre of Melbourne. The city is set out in a simple grid pattern.

Below: *With the gold rushes of the 1850s, Melbourne became the cultural and financial centre of Australia. Today, its modern high-rise buildings are a reminder that this city beside the Yarra is still a vital commercial centre.*

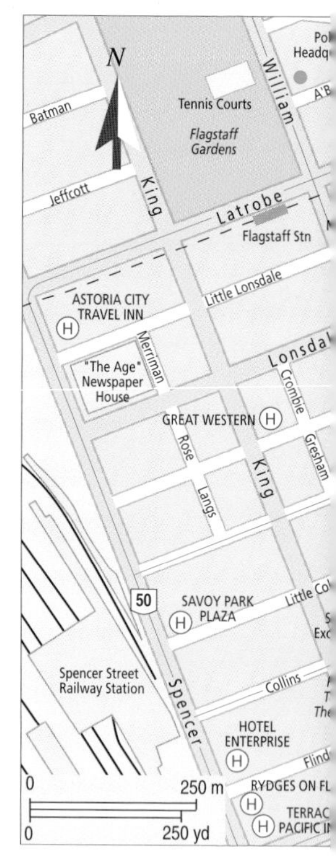

City Sightseeing

The central business district is unique in the way it blends the Victorian architecture of the city's boom period with modern high-rise buildings. This is not an accidental design decision. As long ago as 1971, committees were formed to plan Melbourne's development to the year 2000. Part of this plan was to strike a balance between modern development and a sense of history.

A sensible starting point is **West Gate Bridge**, which rises 54m (177ft) above the Yarra River, and offers a fine panorama of the city, as does the view from the restaurant on the 35th floor of the **Regent Hotel** in Collins Street.

Other ways of seeing the city include hot-air ballooning, canoeing at Albert Park Lake and taking a cruise across Port Phillip Bay.

The city centre is notable for its wide range of historic buildings. The **Block Arcade**, which dates from 1892, is a fine example of a Victorian shopping arcade. The **Rialto Building**, at 497 Collins Street, is a marvellous Italian Gothic building symbolic of the

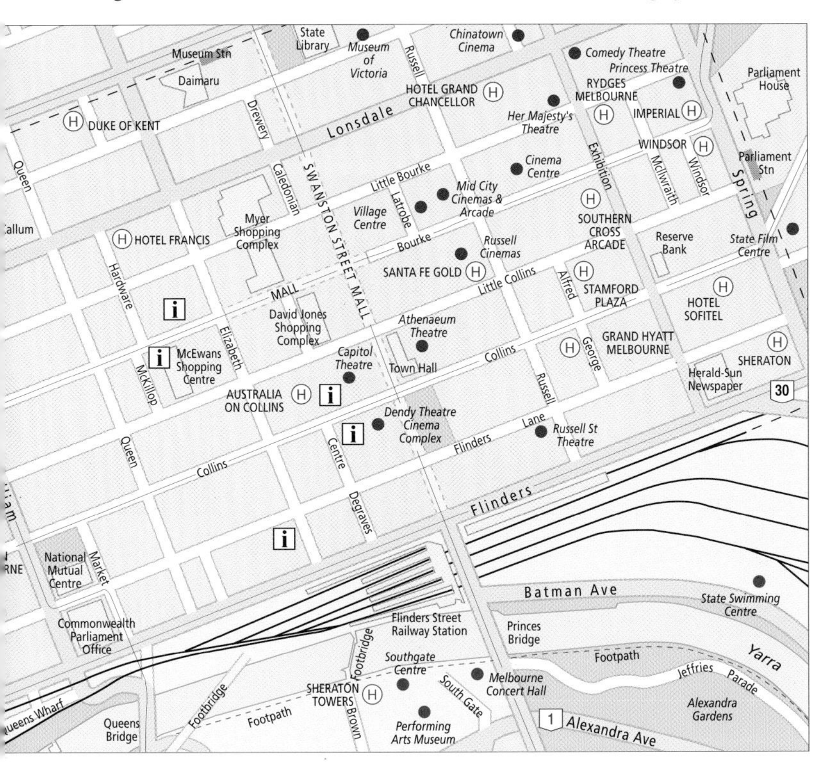

affluence of the 1890s, and the **Royal Arcade** (1869), at 331 Bourke Street, is a reminder of the wealth that flowed into the city after the gold rushes at Bendigo and Ballarat.

Shopping

Melbourne is regarded, certainly by Victorians, as the best shopping centre in Australia. **Bourke Street**, **Collins Street**, the Block Arcade off Collins Street and the Royal Arcade off Bourke Street are noted for their elegant, expensive boutiques.

Beyond the city centre are **Toorak Road** (the road of the city's elite, with a selection of expensive boutiques and clothing shops), and **Chapel Street** with its attractive, specialist boutiques.

Things to Do

No visit to Melbourne is complete without experiencing the **Yarra River**. It is possible to enjoy picnics on the banks. It is also possible to hire canoes, to sit in restaurants which are moored along the banks, to go cycling along the **Yarra River Cycle Track** or to join a variety of cruises, many of which serve delicious food and wine.

Melbourne is home to **Australian Rules Football**. Visitors during the football season should not miss out on this unique and fast-moving game. It is a strange combination of rugby, soccer and Gaelic football and has almost become the state's religion.

People interested in the history of Melbourne can join any number of organised **Heritage Walks** around the city or purchase Heritage Walk brochures and explore historic sites at their own pace.

Melbourne is now the only major Australian city which still operates a wide-ranging **tram service**. This delightful form of transportation is an integral part of city life. It is possible to buy a day ticket and to use the trams to explore the city's central business district as well as the suburbs.

Eating

Melbourne is noted for the diversity and quality of its cuisine. The city boasts excellent Asian restaurants, superb French nouvelle cuisine and European ethnic eateries. Still, there is nothing to compare with the concentration of Italian restaurants on **Lygon Street**. The *Age Good Food Guide* is an annual publication which lists restaurants according to the style of cuisine.

Parks, Gardens, Museums and Galleries

The city has excellent parks, notably the **Royal Botanic Gardens** and the **King's Domain Gardens**, with **La Trobe Cottage** (1839) and the **Shrine of Remembrance**, and **Fitzroy Gardens** with **Captain Cook's Cottage** which was transported from its original location in Yorkshire.

The **Arts Centre of Victoria** includes the superb **National Gallery of Victoria** which has one of the country's best collections of Australian art. The front façade with its water walls is breathtaking.

Around Victoria

Although it is a small state, Victoria is diverse and unusual. It offers both the snowfields of the **Snowy Mountains** and the deserts of the **Wimmera** and **Mallee**; and the spectacular formations which draw people to the **Great Ocean Road** as well as the old gold-mining towns of **Stawell, Bendigo** and **Ballarat**.

The Central Highlands

Lying to the north-west of Melbourne is Victoria's Central Highlands. The region was settled in the 1830s by about 70 squatters who turned the land into one of Australia's most productive fat lamb and wool areas.

In 1851, gold was found at the tiny settlement of Clunes. In the next year, gold was discovered at over 20 sites in the highlands and gold fever brought tens of thousands of new settlers to the area. Once the initial excitement and the possibility of picking nuggets of gold from the ground began to wane, the area returned to agriculture.

Public Gardens

- **Royal Botanic Gardens** – open Mon–Sat, Oct–Mar 07:00-sunset: Apr– Sep, 07:30–sunset. Sundays and Public holidays, Sep–Apr 08:30–sunset; May–Aug features flowerbeds, trees, lawns and lakes. The **National Herbarium** has a large collection of dried plants including some of those gathered by Joseph Banks during Captain Cook's voyage to Australia in 1770.
- **King's Domain Gardens** include Victoria's first Government House and the current residence. Tours of Government House occur on Monday, Wednesday and Saturday. Bookings, tel: (03) 9654-5528/9654-4711.
- **Treasury Gardens** – grassy lawns and old shady trees. There is a memorial to John F Kennedy beside the lake.
- **Flagstaff Gardens** – a beautiful terraced garden overlooking Port Phillip Bay.

Opposite: *Melbourne's substantial Chinese community is one of the legacies of the gold-rush era. Today, Chinatown in Little Bourke Street offers the visitor a wide range of Chinese and South-East Asian cuisine.*

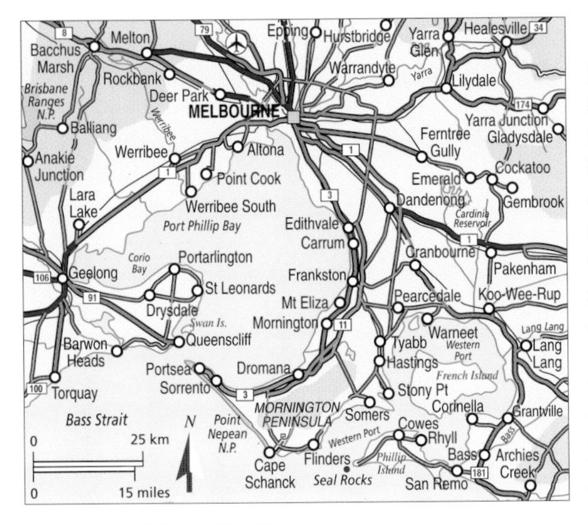

Although **Ballarat** and **Bendigo** both have an important industrial sector the biggest growth industry is tourism. The jewel of the area's tourism is found at **Sovereign Hill**, where an 1850s gold-mining town has been convincingly recreated.

Ballarat has a Gold Museum, a memorial to the **Eureka Stockade** and a **Fine Art Gallery** which has an exceptional collection of Australian paintings.

Sovereign Hill

Sovereign Hill's main street evokes a mining town's ambience. There is also a Government Camp with an officers' quarters, a court-house and military barracks. It is easy to spend a day at this impressive recreation of a 19th-century gold-mining town. You can pan for gold (and actually get small nuggets), inspect the various shops, watch the blacksmith at work and, at night, watch the spectacular 'Blood on the Southern Cross', a recreation of the Eureka Stockade riot.

Right: *Bendigo still possesses much of the charm and grace which made it one of Victoria's great 19th-century gold-mining towns. At the centre of the town are the beautiful Conservatory Gardens.*

Left: *Sovereign Hill is one of Victoria's premier attractions. Located at Ballarat, this remarkable 'village' is a total re-creation of a 19th-century gold-mining town with shops, pubs, mining facilities and even a horse-drawn stagecoach.*

Gippsland

To the east of Melbourne lies Gippsland, encompassing an area which stretches from **Western Port** around **Wilsons Promontory** and north along the coast to the New South Wales border.

The Great Dividing Range is a real challenge. This seemingly inhospitable, heavily forested area is sparsely populated even today. It falls away sharply to the plains which stretch across to **Ninety Mile Beach** and encompass the lakes which lie between Bairnsdale and Sale.

In the 1860s, with the major goldfields in the Central Highlands nearly exhausted, Government surveyors moved into the Gippsland area hoping to find fields which would keep the itinerant miners in Victoria.

The area was never a truly successful gold-mining region. About as close as gold fever ever came was the town of Walhalla, where gold was discovered in 1862.

Access to Melbourne as a result of the construction of a railway line saw the rapid expansion of dairying in the area and by the 1930s, Gippsland had become Melbourne's major supplier of dairy produce.

The real economic wealth of the state of Victoria lies in its coal deposits. Since 1824, it had been known that coal existed in Gippsland.

Bendigo

Bendigo's gold-rush days have left it with an unusual range of attractions including a **Chinese joss house**, a number of **wineries** and the **Central Deborah Mine** which was continuously mined for over a century, yielding an extraordinary 690 million grams (over 240 million ounces) of gold. **Sandhurst Town**, 12km (7 miles) out of Bendigo, is a local equivalent of Sovereign Hill.

Gippsland

Victoria has traditionally had a strong industrial base. Gippsland, for example, is the centre of Victoria's coal and power industries, and cities like Morwell provide the state with both locally manufactured coal briquettes and electricity from the Yallourn Power Station. An added economic impetus occurred in the 1960s, when the Esso–sBHP consortium discovered oil and gas off the coast. This find now supplies most of the country.

Above: *The Snowy Mountains, Australia's favourite ski destination, are only a few hours north of Melbourne. In winter Victorians travel to popular resorts such as Mt Buller to enjoy the snow.*

North-eastern Victoria

From Swan Hill on the Murray River across to the Snowy Mountains and their numerous ski resorts, the north-eastern region of Victoria is characterised by great diversity. To the east the region is mountainous and experiences snow and sub-zero temperatures during winter. The mountains fall away to gently undulating slopes and by Swan Hill it is monotonously flat.

Gold was discovered as early as 1845, but it wasn't until the serious gold rushes of the 1850s that the fossickers and miners moved into the area. The first major discovery occurred at **Beechworth** in 1852.

Myrtleford to the south is another town which boomed during the 1850s and waned until after World War II, when large numbers of migrants, mostly from Italy, Spain and Yugoslavia, arrived in the area and established a number of tobacco and hop farms and walnut orchards.

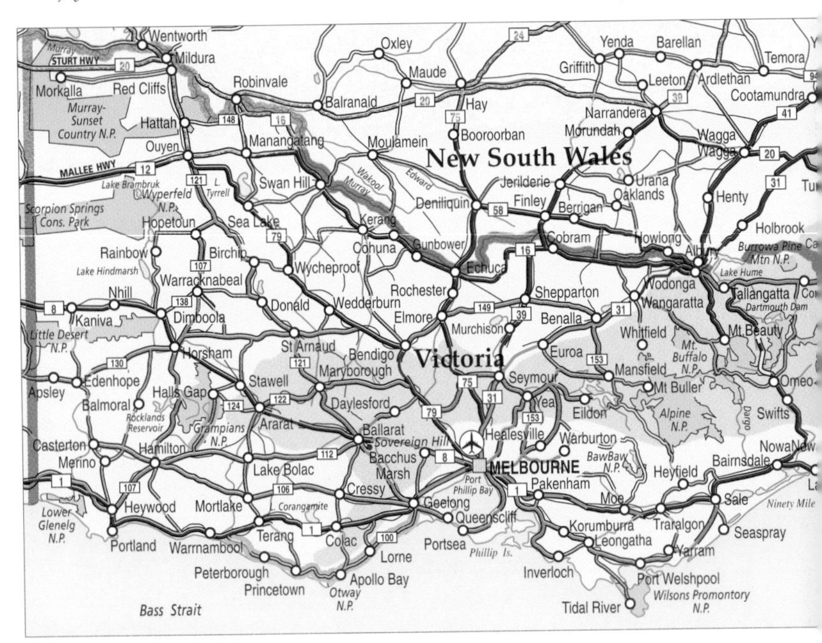

Similarly **Rutherglen**, once a gold town with a population of 25,000, is now known as the centre of viticulture. It has an annual wine festival, viticulture college and Vinegrowers Association.

Yackandandah, with its tiny population of under 500, is now entirely classified by the National Trust and consequently relies upon tourism to sustain it. At its height it supported 3000 miners, many of whom had travelled from the North American goldfields.

Beyond the gold towns are the Murray River towns of **Swan Hill**, **Echuca**, **Yarrawonga** and **Wodonga**.

The first paddle steamer from South Australia reached Swan Hill in 1853, and the following year port facilities were established at Wodonga. Today, the romantic riverboat past is recaptured with paddle steamer journeys down the Murray. The huge *Murray River Queen* cruises from Swan Hill to Goolwa in South Australia.

GREAT OCEAN ROAD

This road was completed in 1932. Before that the seaside resorts of Lorne and Apollo Bay were accessible only by narrow inland roads. The Great Ocean Road was built as a memorial to those who died in World War I and it took 15 years to complete. Everyone who worked on the road was an ex-serviceman. It starts at Torquay and skirts the coast to Peterborough. The road is one of the most magnificent coastal journeys in Australia and one of the great attractions of Victoria.

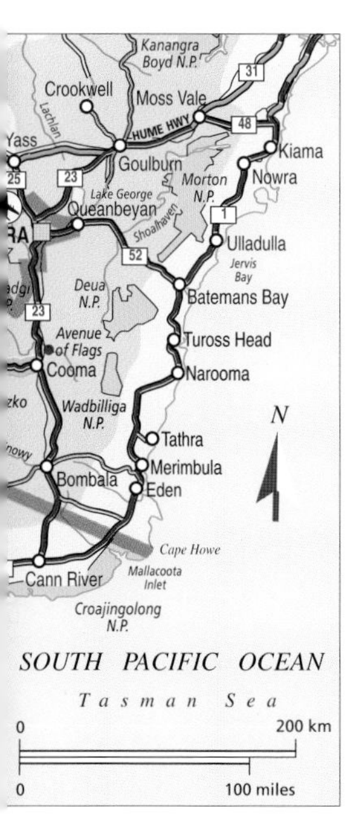

THE WESTERN DISTRICT

Along the southern coast of Victoria, from Port Phillip Bay to the South Australian border, is the western district. It includes the major regional centres of **Geelong, Portland**, **Port Fairy** and **Warrnambool**.

The highlight of the area is the **Great Ocean Road**, a winding coastal route which provides the traveller with superb ocean views. **London Bridge** and the **Twelve Apostles**, rock formations off the coast, are much photographed scenic wonders.

The area to the north-west of the Grampians is dry, marginal country which is good for wheat growing and sheep grazing. The Wimmera was settled by squatters in the 1830s, and settlement of the Mallee occurred about a decade later. The small, though reliable, rainfall in the Wimmera allowed for the development of wheat and sheep industries.

The towns, most of which are service centres for the pastoral areas, have tried to strengthen their fragile economic bases by establishing small, rural industries like canneries, meat-freezing works and flour mills.

Melbourne and Victoria at a Glance

Best Times To Visit

September to **November** (spring) new growth brings the city alive after the cold winter. **December** to **February** (summer) warm days make exploring Victoria a joy.

Melbourne is known for its changeable weather so be prepared for cool weather, even in summer.

Getting There

Melbourne's **international** and **domestic airport** (Tullamarine) is 22km (14 miles) north-east of the city centre. The Tullamarine freeway makes it a fairly quick trip. **Skybus** shuttle service runs every half hour between the airport and Franklin St depot in the city. Like all big airports it caters well for the international traveller.

Many **car rental** firms have desks at both the international and domestic terminals.

Taxis are also available.

The major bus company, **Greyhound/ Pioneer**, tel: 132030, has an extensive network for interstate travellers. Interstate train travel is easy and frequent, for information and bookings, tel: (03) 9619-5000.

Getting Around

Melbourne's public transport, the **Met**, is an integrated system incorporating bus, suburban railway and the famous **trams**. Trams are the cornerstone of the public transport system and are easy to use.

Melbourne is laid out in a grid pattern, north–south, east–west and the trams run accordingly. The **Met Information Centre** will help with any queries, tel: (03) 9617-0900. They are open from 07:00–20:55.

Taxis in the city are readily available and car rental firms are well represented.

Where to Stay

Melbourne's city centre is quite small but is well catered for with excellent accommodation. The tram system makes staying just out of the central business district very easy. There are hundreds of hotels, motels and serviced apartments to choose from.

All Seasons Premier Swanston Hotel, Swanston St, convenient location, apartment-style rooms with modern facilities, ideal for families, tel: (03) 9663-4711, fax: 9663-7447.

Banks Hotel, Cnr Spencer & Flinders sts, well appointed small hotel in the heart of the financial district, tel: (03) 9663-4711, fax: 9663-8191.

Le Meridien Melbourne, Collins St, 19th-century hotel with style, comfort and elegance, centrally located, tel: (03) 9620-9111, fax: 9614-1219.

Stamford Plaza on Little Collins St, luxurious serviced apartments in the centre of the city, tel: (03) 9659-1000, fax: 9659-0999.

Rockmans Regency, cnr Exhibition & Lonsdale sts, small elegant boutique hotel located in the centre of the theatre district, tel: (03) 9662-3900, fax: 9663-4297.

Windsor Hotel, Spring St, beautiful old world hotel classified by the National Trust (1883), blends tradition with modern luxury, tel: (03) 9653-0653, fax: 9633-6001.

Budget Accommodation

Batman Hill Hotel, Spencer St, centrally located behind Spencer St Railway Station, excellent city hotel, priced well, tel: (03) 9614-6344, fax: 9614-1189.

Birches Boutique Apartments, Simpson St, fully appointed serviced apartments, walking distance to the city centre, tel: (03) 9417-2344, fax: 9417-5872.

Hotel Grand Chancellor, Lonsdale St, good service and facilities at a reasonable rate at this centrally located hotel, tel: (03) 9663-3161, fax 9662-3479.

Magnolia Court Hotel, Powlett St, originally built in 1858, offers intimate atmosphere, tel: (03) 9419-4222, fax: 9416-0841.

Riverside Apartments, cnr Flinders St & Highlander Lane, centrally located serviced

Melbourne and Victoria at a Glance

apartments with panoramic views over the city, tel: (03) 9283-7633, fax: 9629-7582.
Treasury Motor Lodge, Powlett St, small reasonably priced motel near Fitzroy Gardens, tel: (03) 9417-5281.

Where to Eat

Melbourne is considered the culinary capital of Australia. The variety of restaurants is extraordinary. There are a number of food guides available to help the confused traveller. *Dining in Melbourne* from the Melbourne Tourism Authority describes the cuisine and includes location maps. *The Age* newspaper also produces a *Good Food Guide* for Melbourne which can be picked up at most local newsagencies.
Colonial Tramcar, enjoy Australian cuisine while travelling in a beautifully renovated tramcar, tel: (03) 9696-4000.
Pavillion St Kilda, St Kilda, seafood at its best served in a beautifully restored bathing pavilion overlooking the bay, tel: (03) 9534-8221.
Malaysian Delight, East Kew, reasonably priced Malaysian food, tel: (03) 9817-2459.
Mietta's, Queenscliff, elegant cuisine served in elegant surrounds of a restored mansion, tel: (03) 5258-1066.
EST, South Melbourne, stylish French cooking, tel: (03) 9690-5628.
Stephanie's, Hawthorn East, award-winning restaurant housed in a restored mansion, tel: (03) 9822-8944.
Thy Thy, Richmond, Vietnamese cooking at its very best, reasonably priced, tel: (03) 9429-1104.

Tours and Excursions

AAT Kings Coaches offer a large selection of coach tours around Melbourne and further afield in modern air-conditioned coaches, tel: (03) 9666-3363.
City Explorer is a double-decker bus which operates hourly from Flinders St Station and calls at the main points of interest around the city.
City River Cruises, MV *Melba Star* gives the sightseer a wonderful one-hour cruise on the Yarra River. Luncheon and dinner service also available, tel: (03) 9650-2214.
Kestral Helicopter Tours offers a variety of helicopter tours, a wonderful way to see Melbourne and its surrounds, tel: (03) 9629-4452.
Melbourne Out and About Heritage Walks offer a conducted historical walk through Melbourne, with informative talks about this beautiful Victorian city and its architecture, tel: (03) 9241-1085.
Steam Tug Wattle – a day out with a difference, this 1933 tug boat lets you explore Port Phillip Bay in style, tel: (03) 9328-2739.

Useful Contacts

Department of Conservation and Environment, manages the state parks and gives helpful information for bushwalkers, tel: (03) 9412-4011.
Information Victoria, Collins St, has a large range of maps and guide books, tel: 1300 366 356.
National Trust of Victoria, Tasman Terrace, has an information centre that can help the traveller explore the history of Melbourne's Victorian past, tel: (03) 9654-4711.
Royal Automobile Club of Victoria, Collins St, large selection of road maps and helpful information, tel: (03) 9607-2137.

MELBOURNE	J	F	M	A	M	J	J	A	S	O	N	D
AVERAGE TEMP. °F	68	68	66	63	57	53	52	53	55	59	63	64
AVERAGE TEMP. °C	20	20	19	17	14	12	11	12	13	15	17	18
Hours of Sun Daily	8	7	6	5	4	3	4	4	5	6	7	7
SEA TEMP. °F	66	66	64	64	60	59	57	55	55	57	59	63
SEA TEMP. °C	19	19	18	18	16	15	14	13	13	14	15	17
RAINFALL in	1.8	1.8	2	2.3	2.3	1.9	1.9	2	2.3	2.7	2.4	2.3
RAINFALL mm	48	48	52	58	58	50	49	51	59	68	60	59
Days of Rainfall	8	7	9	12	14	14	15	16	15	14	12	11

5
Hobart and Tasmania

Tasmania is the smallest of Australia's states, yet it is an area of great and undiscovered beauty.

The island is the most mountainous of Australia's states. Subject to extensive glaciation during the last ice age, the southern coastline, which has no settlements, is a series of rugged, inaccessible cliffs.

The centre of the island is a plateau with glacial lakes and a number of major mountains, most notably **Mount Ossa**, **Ben Lomond**, **Cradle Mountain** and **Eldon Park**. All rise above 1400m (4600ft).

Most of the island's mountainous terrain remains in its natural state, its agricultural land being concentrated along the north coast and in the valleys of the **Tamar, Derwent** and **Huon rivers**.

For decades, the apple was the symbol for the state, firstly because the island's shape is similar to an apple and secondly, because, for many Australians, apples were the only product they associated with Tasmania.

Tasmanian fauna and flora is of unique importance. The Huon pine can grow for over 2000 years. The Tasmanian devil, once an inhabitant of mainland Australia, is now restricted to the island and the Tasmanian tiger is still thought to be hiding in the state's wilderness.

DON'T MISS

*** **Port Arthur:** remnants of Australia's convict past.
* **Queenstown:** a moonscape produced by mining and pollution
*** **Cradle Lake:** marvellous, dramatic wilderness.
** **The Nut at Stanley:** strange north coast outcrop.
*** **Ross and Richmond:** beautifully preserved 19th-century villages.
*** **Battery Point** and **Salamanca Place:** old world charm in Hobart.

Hobart

Unique among the state capitals, Hobart has a strong sense of its colonial, 19th-century heritage.

Named after Robert Hobart, Secretary of State for War and the Colonies at the time of its settlement, it is

Opposite: *The Russell Falls Nature Walk is a half hour stroll through stands of stringybark, mountain ash and white gum.*

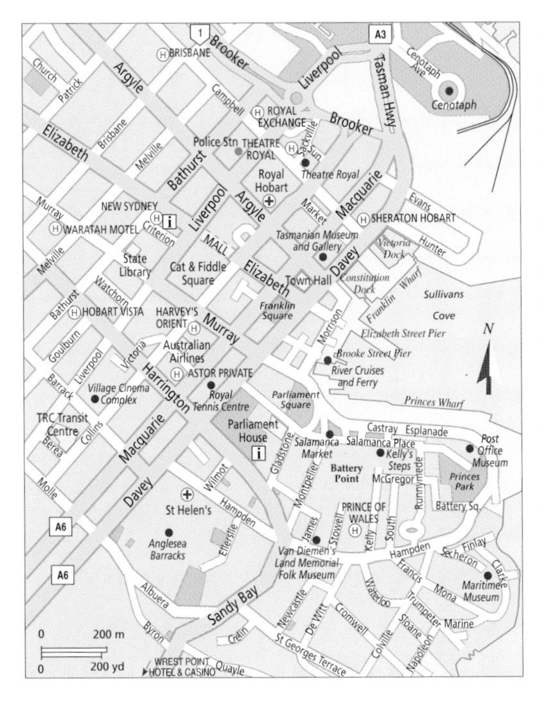

Tasmania's chief port. It is protected from the worst of the island's weather, which occurs on Tasmania's rugged west coast.

The city lies on either side of the Derwent River and is partially protected by Mount Wellington in the west and Mount Nelson to the south.

Hobart's location on the Derwent, its straggling, irregular appearance, and the distinctive old world charm of its docklands and port have often been written about in glowing terms. The dockside warehouses at Salamanca Place are fine examples of this.

Hobart had inauspicious beginnings. Its sole *raison d'être* was to keep the French out of Australia. By 1827 it had an estimated population of 5000. In recent times, tourism to the city has increased significantly, fuelled by the establishment of Australia's first legal casino, The Wrest Point Hotel–Casino. The casino, with its distinctive 64m (210ft) high cylindrical tower, is at Sandy Bay.

Opposite: *One of Hobart's great attractions is the Royal Tasmanian Botanical Gardens which lie on the banks of the Derwent River, just beyond Government House.*

CLIMATE

Hobart has an average annual rainfall of 630mm (25in) and a temperature range from a summer monthly average of 21°C (70°F) in February, to a winter monthly average of 11°C (52°F) in July. It often snows in winter.

City Sightseeing

The Royal Tasmanian Botanical Gardens ★★

In 1826, with the widespread agreement that Hobart Town should be the capital of Van Diemen's Land, Governor Arthur had plans drawn up for Government House and an adjoining Botanical Gardens on the banks of the Derwent. Over the next five years, plants were imported from England and over 150 native species were collected from Mount Wellington. The gardens grew progressively during the 19th century.

An excellent map and comprehensive history of the gardens is provided in the brochure *Let's Talk About The Royal Tasmanian Botanical Gardens.* It gives details about the historic Arthur Wall (built by Governor Arthur in 1829), the Rossbank Observatory site (built by Governor Franklin in 1840), the Conservatory, Rosarium, Floral Clock, Fern House and Tropical Glasshouse.

Battery Point ★★★

No other Australian city has an area to equal Battery Point. It is a very elegant 'suburb' with an extraordinary concentration of beautifully preserved 19th-century houses.

The only way to experience Battery Point is to walk up Kelly's Steps from **Salamanca Place** and start wandering through the winding streets. Battery Point gets its name from the battery of guns which were mounted on the headland in 1818.

It was around this time that building started with Stowell and Secheron House (built around 1831 and located at 21 Secheron Road) and the construction of the impressive warehouses in Salamanca Place.

By 1850, Salamanca Place and Battery Point had become the maritime focal point of the city. Sailors came from all over the world and sailors' and workers' cottages were built in an area which was already noted for its gracious Georgian mansions. In this sense, Battery Point is a unique combination of living styles. Neat, tiny cottages owned by working people stand next to mansions in a streetscape which includes roads and even 'village greens' designed to mimic the streets of rural and urban England.

The most impressive and famous building in Battery Point is **St George's Church,** built from 1836 to 1838. It is regarded as the finest Greek Revival Church in Australia.

It is fun to explore Battery Point, enjoying the sense of surprise offered by the whole area. If you want something a little more organised, the National Trust offers conducted walking tours on Saturday mornings.

Highlights of Battery Point

- **St George's Church:** built between 1836 and 1838, regarded as the finest Greek Revival Church in Australia with its impressive Doric portico and decorative carvings.
- **Barton Cottage:** at 72 Hampden Road built in 1837 by Captain William Wilson and now bed and breakfast accommodation.
- **Colville Cottage:** (1877) at 32 Mona Street.
- **Cromwell Cottage:** (1880) at 6 Cromwell Street.
- **Tantallon Lodge:** (1906) at 8 Mona Street.

The National Trust offers conducted walking tours on Saturday mornings.

Right: *Located on the Derwent River, Hobart retains much of its 19th-century charm. This view from Mount Nelson, with the Wrest Point Hotel–Casino in the foreground, captures the beauty of this small city.*

Historic Buildings in the City

The pamphlet *Let's Talk About Hobart's Historic Buildings* concentrates on the important historic buildings and sites in the city's central business district. The visitor can see most of the important buildings by completing a circuit from the City Hall up Macquarie Street to Harrington Street then down towards Salamanca Place and back along Davey Street.

The buildings of particular note include the **Commissariat Store** (1808–10) at 40 Macquarie Street (Hobart's oldest building), the **Bond Store** (1824) behind the Commissariat, the **Tasmanian Museum and Art Gallery** (1863) and the **Town Hall**, with its impressive ballroom, which was built in 1864.

Of particular note is the **Theatre Royal** at 29 Campbell Street, which was built in 1837 and is recognised as the oldest theatre in Australia. The stage has been trod by such theatrical luminaries as Laurence Olivier and Noel Coward.

Anglesea Barracks **

Further up Davey Street are the **Anglesea Barracks**. Built in 1814, they are recognised as the oldest military establishment still in use in Australia. Any tour of the barracks should include the Guard House (1838), the Hospital (1818), the Military Gaol (1846), the Officers' Quarters (1814) and the Old Drill Hall (1824).

SALAMANCA PLACE

Every year, the victorious yacht which has led the fleet from Sydney in the Sydney–Hobart Ocean Yacht Race arrives at Salamanca Place. Each weekend, locals and visitors mingle in the excellent Salamanca Markets. And, it is at Salamanca Place that the Georgian warehouses (built between 1830 and 1850) have been converted into excellent restaurants, galleries, craft and gift shops. It is widely recognised that these are the finest dockside Georgian warehouses remaining in Australia.

Mount Wellington **

Towering over the city is Mount Wellington, a dormant volcano which is 1270m (4165ft) high. On Christmas Day 1798, George Bass became the first European to climb the mountain and to enjoy the spectacular view across the Derwent River and down the D'Entrecasteaux Channel.

It has become one of the major sites of Hobart and, over the years, it has been climbed by such famous people as Charles Darwin and the novelist Anthony Trollope who, having climbed it in 1872, rather haughtily described it as 'just enough of a mountain to give excitement to ladies and gentlemen'.

Boat trips to the Cadburys factory **

The *Derwent Explorer* departs from the Brooke Street Pier, Franklin Wharf, and makes its way up-river to the Cadburys factory at Claremont where, apart from the educational interest of seeing chocolate being produced, the visitor gets an opportunity to sample and purchase the product.

A number of other cruises are available which go around the harbour, down the Derwent and through the D'Entrecasteaux Channel.

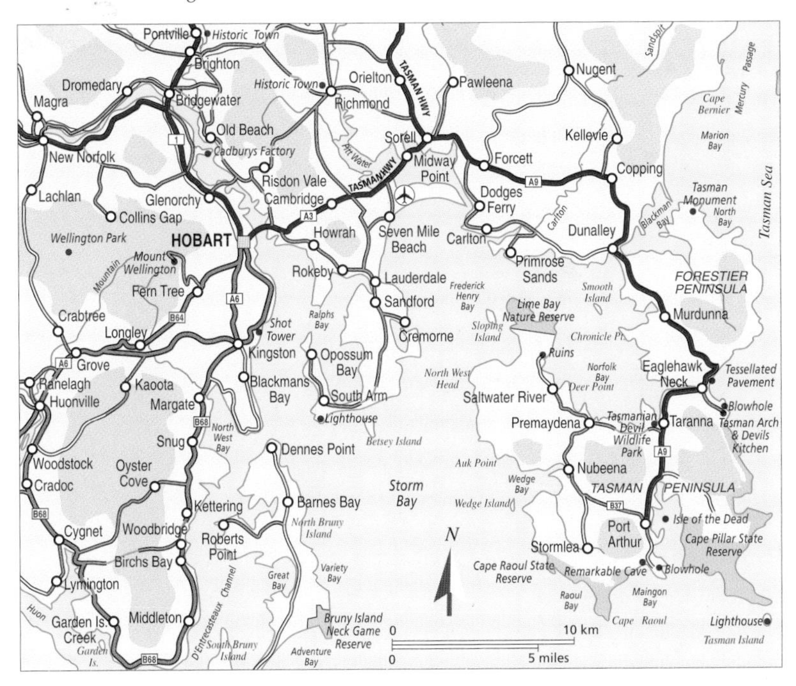

Boat Harbour

Located 183km (113 miles) north-west of Launceston, Boat Harbour may well be the most beautiful place on the whole north coast of Tasmania. This charming village, located on the side of a gentle hill which tumbles down to a superb white beach with rocky headlands on either side, looks like a picture off a chocolate box or a scenic calendar. The sea is bright green and blue, the beach very clean, the surroundings delightful, and the village is sleepy and peaceful.

This Week in Tasmania, a free guide widely available in hotels and tourist offices in Hobart, offers an extensive overview to restaurants, hotels and motels in the city centre. The restaurants around **Constitution Dock** are essential for anyone wanting to enjoy reasonably priced and deliciously fresh seafood.

From Hobart to Launceston

The most important pastoral area in Tasmania lies in the valley which has been created by the confluence of the South Esk, Macquarie and Tamar rivers. This rich, flat valley which has Launceston as its main centre, and is traversed by the main north–south road which joins Launceston and Hobart, is the most important wool- and beef-growing area in the state.

The drive from Hobart to Launceston is a rare opportunity to experience what Australia must have been like in the 19th century. Villages such as **Ross** and **Richmond** have been preserved and, although they are now the focus of the tourist industry, it is easy to appreciate their original charm with a little stretch of the imagination.

Tasmania's second major centre is **Launceston**. With a population of approximately 68,000 it has retained the ambience of a large country town. Launceston is an attractive and important centre with a large number of historic buildings. The enthusiastic tourist could easily spend a day exploring the city. Of particular note are the **Gorge**, a popular swimming and picnicking location, the **Penny Royal**, a tourist attraction which includes Ritchie's Mill Art Centre and an old **tramway**, and the **harbour**.

The North and East Coasts

The north-west coastal strip, running from **Smithton** and **Stanley** across to **Devonport**, is acknowledged as the best land on the island. The soils are rich and volcanic, and climatic conditions are ideal for the raising of beef and dairy cattle (the area is known for its cheeses and prime quality beef) and the growing of potatoes and peas.

The northern and north-eastern coastal strip from Devonport across the estuary of the Tamar River to **Scottsdale** and **Gladstone** and around the coast to **St Helens** and **Scamander** is heavily cropped. The area produces substantial harvests of potatoes, wheat and barley.

This entire coast is worth exploring. It has not been overdeveloped and, when the weather is good, to walk up **The Nut** at Stanley or marvel at the beauty of the windswept beaches at **Boat Harbour** (surely one of the loveliest places on the entire island) or **Penguin**, is to experience the intense beauty of this lovely region.

Left: *Coles Bay and Freycinet National Park, on Tasmania's east coast, offer visitors the opportunity to fish in the waters of Great Oyster Bay, to walk in the park and climb the Hazards or the mountains to the south, both of which offer marvellous views across Wine Glass Bay and out across the Tasman Sea.*

King Island to the north-west of Tasmania has an extraordinary reputation for dairy products. It is believed that the island's pastures have grown from seeds in matresses washed up after shipwrecks. King Island butters, cheeses and creams are found in delicatessens on the mainland and have become a byword for quality.

The West Coast

The West Coast is wild, windy, rainy and isolated. It is a mixture of the magical and the bizarre. The whole area can be summed up by **Macquarie Harbour** and the small town of Strahan.

Strahan, on the edge of the unspoilt beauty of Macquarie Harbour, is the last outpost of civilization on the west coast and surely one of the loneliest places on earth. The British created this place to be the ultimate penal colony. Named after Governor Lachlan Macquarie, the 50km (31 mile) long harbour opens to the sea through the narrow, eddying waters of Hells Gates and receives the waters from the **King** and **Gordon rivers**.

It was established in 1821, and closed down in 1833, when the convicts were all removed to **Port Arthur** on the east coast. The prisoners worked on a nearby coal seam and rowed across the harbour each day to cut down the large stands of Huon pine which edged the waterways.

Cradle Mountain

Located 144km (90 miles) from Launceston and 83km (50 miles) from Devonport, Cradle Mountain is the central feature of the Cradle Mountain–Lake St Clair National Park, part of Tasmania's World Heritage area. The park covers an area of 124,942ha (309,000 acres) which is characterised by a rugged, glaciated landscape with over 25 major peaks and a wide range of glacial formations – tarns, glacial lakes, moraine deposits, U-shaped valleys and waterfalls.

The area was glaciated during the last ice age (about 10,000 years ago) when a huge 6km (4 mile) ice cap formed and glaciers flowed from its edges, carving the landscape into dramatic shapes with their inexorable erosive powers. The park offers many superb walks.

It was from here that the notorious convict, Alexander Pearce, attempted to escape in 1822. Pearce and seven other convicts sought to cross the island to Hobart where they hoped they could catch a merchant ship and escape to some ill-defined freedom. However, they lost their way and, in the ensuing weeks, all of the escapees disappeared except for Pearce. When he was recaptured, unproven accusations of cannibalism were made against him. The following year Pearce escaped again, accompanied by another convict, Thomas Cox. Once again Pearce found himself without food and, to solve the problem, he killed and ate Cox. When he was finally recaptured Pearce admitted to eating Cox and confessed to cannibalism during his first escape. He was subsequently executed in Hobart.

The harbour remains virtually untouched. On a clear day it is like a near-perfect mirror. Its waters are stained by the brown button grass which grows on the river banks and its shores are heavily wooded. Taking a trip across the harbour and entering the **Franklin–Gordon Wild Rivers National Park** is one of the essential trips in western Tasmania.

The west coast is also a major mining area. In 1871, a man known to everyone as 'Philosopher' Smith discovered tin at Mount Bischoff. In the next decade, substantial deposits of silver were found at Zeehan, Waratah, Dundas and Farrell; copper was found at Mount Lyell and Queenstown; tin was discovered at Mount Cameron, Renison Bell and Thomas's Plains; and goldfields were established at Queenstown, Beaconsfield and along the banks of the Pieman River.

Queenstown, its hills stripped of timber to fire the local copper smelters and permanently denuded by the sulphurous fumes which belch from the smelters, is a surreal nightmare. Its river is polluted and it has the appearance of a deserted moonscape. Yet beyond the reaches of its devastation lie undulating hills covered in morning mist, skies heavy with the dark, low clouds which are such a distinctive part of the climate of the western coast. It is like no other place on earth and a must for those interested in seeing what pollution can do to a beautiful area.

South of Hobart

In recent times, Tasmania has become a popular retreat for people wishing to practice an alternative lifestyle. The **Huon Valley** and the rural areas around Hobart have been settled by potters, woodworkers and craftspeople who sell their wares in the gift shops which have sprung up in the city centre. A round trip from Hobart through Snug and Cygnet and Huonville is a reminder that there are still places on earth which have not been spoilt by modernisation and industrialisation.

It is in the south of Hobart, that the bulk of the state's famous apples are grown as well as apricots and lucrative crops of oil poppies and hops.

Opposite: *Recognised as the finest convict ruins in Australia, Port Arthur is one of Tasmania's premier tourist attractions. The historic church, which stands on the hill above the prison, is without a roof or windows.*

Port Arthur ***

Most remarkable of all the places in Tasmania, and a place definitely not to be missed, is Port Arthur. This magnificently preserved penal colony is a powerful reminder of Australia's early history. About 100km (62 miles) from Hobart, and isolated from the rest of the island by a narrow sliver of land known as Eaglehawk Neck, 12,500 of the most hardened criminals were sent to Port Arthur between 1830 and 1877. And, just to compound the misery in the area, from 1834 to 1849, a special prison for juveniles was in operation across the bay at Port Puer.

The prison at Port Arthur has been magnificently preserved and it is the best opportunity to experience Australia's convict past.

The great challenge for the visitor to Port Arthur is to try to imagine what the settlement was like in the 1850s and 1860s. Anthony Trollope has left us a rather glowing description of a place which has 'the appearance of a large, well-built, clean village with various factories, breweries, and the like'. It is also hard to imagine that by the 1850s Port Arthur was a remarkably self-sufficient settlement and that the convicts were involved in industries as diverse as ship building, growing vegetables, making shoes and boots, manufacturing clothing, making bricks and cutting and processing timber.

Most visitors to Port Arthur include the ferry trip across to the **Isle of the Dead** as part of their itinerary. It became the burial place for Port Arthur residents in 1831 (only months after the establishment of the settlement) and almost immediately was divided into free settler and convict burial grounds.

Don't Miss – Port Arthur

*** **The Penitentiary:** reputedly the largest building in Australia when it was completed in 1844.
** **The Model Prison:** Designed by the Royal Engineers and built with convict labour in 1848, based on the model of Pentonville Gaol in London.
** **Hospital:** substantial ruins, originally built in 1842 and once housed up to 80 ill convicts.
*** **The Isle of the Dead:** burial place for Port Arthur. Over the years, a total of 1769 convicts and 180 free persons were buried on this isolated island.

Hobart and Tasmania at a Glance

Best Times To Visit

September to **November** (spring) Tasmania is alive with new growth and blooms. Fruit trees and spring flowers carpet the countryside.
December to **February** (summer) long twilight evenings in ideal temperate conditions allow for extended exploration of Tasmania. Spring and summer have warm days and cool nights. Although winter can be mild it does come with rainy and unreliable weather and snow on the highlands.

Getting There

Hobart's **Airport** is 26km (16 miles) east of Hobart. **Redline Coach** runs a pick-up and drop-off service between the airport and the city centre.
Ansett and **Australian Airlines** have flights to Tasmania from most Australian state capitals.

If you want a more leisurely journey, or want to take a car to the island, the ***Spirit of Tasmania***, a ferry which is more like a luxury cruise ship, departs from the TT terminal at Melbourne's Station Pier to Devonport's Esplanade at 18:00 on alternate days. The trip takes 14 to 15 hours. For more information ring TT Line, tel: 1800 030 344 toll free.
Qantas, tel: 131313, operates an extensive network of domestic flights.

Getting Around

Car rental is the most popular form of transportation around Tasmania. Distances are short and rail services are limited. There are many car rental firms in Hobart; your hotel or motel will be able to recommend a suitable firm to meet your budget requirements.
Buses within the city of Hobart are run by Metro and are fast and efficient. Visitors wanting to travel around Tasmania should contact the three main bus companies – Redline Coaches, Hobart Coaches and Tasmanian Wilderness Transport. Weekend bus services are infrequent. **Taxis** are readily available.

Where to Stay

There are many fine hotels in Hobart itself. The island is also known for its excellent guest house and bed and breakfast accommodation.
Innkeepers Lenna of Hobart, Runnymede St, Victorian charm with modern conveniences, overlooking the Derwent River, tel: (03) 6223-2911, fax: 6224-0112.
Salamanca Inn, Gladstone St, modern hotel integrated among the old warehouses, well located, tel: (03) 6223-3300, fax: 6223-7167.
Hotel Grand Chancellor, Davey St, first-class hotel with all the comforts,tel: (03) 6235-4535, fax: 6223-8175.
Wrest Point Hotel–Casino, Sandy Bay Rd, first-class hotel and casino with riverside views, tel: (03) 6225-0112, fax: 6225-2424.

Budget Accommodation
Battery Point Guest House, 'Mandalay', McGregor St, attractive converted coach house and stables, tel: (03) 6224-2111.
Fountainside Motor Inn, Cnr Brooker Hwy & Liverpool St, modern motel, reasonably priced, central location, tel: (03) 6234-2911, fax: 6231-0710.
Sandy Bay Motor Inn, Sandy Bay Rd, near casino, reasonably priced, modern accommodation, tel: (03) 6225-2511, fax: 6225-4354.

Launceston
Tasmania's second-largest city, situated at the head of the Tamar River. Launceston is known as the Garden City. Accommodation is plentiful and varied.
Great Northern Hotel, 3 Earl St, beautifully appointed near parks and city centre, tel: (03) 6331-9999, fax: 6331-3712.
Novotel Launceston, Cameron St, elegant, centrally located hotel with all amenities, tel: (03) 6334-3434, fax: 6331-7347.

Hobart and Tasmania at a Glance

Budget Accommodation

Old Bakery Inn, York St, restored old inn (1870), a member of Historic Hotels Australia, tel: (03) 6331-7900, fax: 6331-7756.

Sandors On the Park, Brisbane St, central location opposite city park, offering quality accommodation, tel: (03) 6331-2055, fax: 6331-5851.

Refer to *This Week in Tasmania*, a free booklet which gives a comprehensive list of restaurants, hotels and entertainment in Hobart. It is readily available in hotels, motels and tourist information offices.

Where to Eat

Restaurants are plentiful in Hobart. Battery Point, the area around the harbour and Salamanca Place are well known for their fine restaurants and brasseries.

Ball & Chain Restaurant, Salamanca Place, steak and seafood house, tel: (03) 6223-2655, fax: 6224-2339.

Alexander's, Battery Point, international food, elegant surroundings, tel: (03) 6232-3900, fax: 6224-0112.

Mures Upper Deck Seafood Restaurant, Victoria Dock, excellent seafood and view, tel: (03) 6231-2121.

The Point Revolving Restaurant, Wrest Point Hotel–Casino, fresh Tasmanian ingredients, served imaginatively, tel: (03) 6225-0112.

Launceston

This Week in Tasmania, provides an extensive list of restaurants in and around Launceston.

The Royal Oak, Brisbane St, bistro-style meals served in this central hotel, dating from the 1800s, tel: (03) 6331-5346.

Shrimps, George St, excellent seafood served in a National Trust building, tel: (03) 6334-0584.

Woofies, Macquarie House, Civic Square, historic building, serving reasonably priced food, tel: (03) 6334-0695.

Tours and Excursions

Most tours and excursions are run from the Tasmanian Travel Centre. Comprehensive lists of coach, self-drive and wilderness tours are available. They will also help you plan your own tour with hotel bookings and 'must see and do' activities, tel: (03) 6230-8233, fax: 6224-0289.

Redline Coaches, the main coach line in Tasmania has many tours throughout the state, tel: (03) 6234-4077.

Tasmanian Wilderness Transport, for the ultimate wilderness holiday, tel: (008) 030-505 toll free.

The most common way to travel around Tasmania is to hire a car or campervan, work out a schedule and pre-book your accommodation.

Useful Contacts

The Tasmanian Travel Centre, 20 Davey St, open week days 08:30 to 17:15, weekends and holidays 09:00 to 13:00, tel: (03) 6230-8233, fax: 6224-0289.

The Royal Automobile Club of Tasmania, cnr Murray and Patrick sts, road maps and advice are part of their service – make sure you have evidence of membership of a similar organisation, tel: (03) 6234-8784, fax: 6234-9784.

The Department of Parks and Wildlife, Macquarie St, essential for would-be walkers, tel: 336191.

HOBART	J	F	M	A	M	J	J	A	S	O	N	D
AVERAGE TEMP. °F	70	70	68	62	57	53	53	55	59	63	64	68
AVERAGE TEMP. °C	21	21	20	17	14	12	12	13	15	17	18	20
Hours of Sun Daily	8	7	6	5	4	4	4	5	6	6	7	7
SEA TEMP. °F	61	62	61	59	57	55	53	52	52	55	55	59
SEA TEMP. °C	16	17	16	15	14	13	12	11	11	13	13	15
RAINFALL in	1.8	1.5	1.8	2	1.9	2.2	2.1	2	2	2.5	2.2	2.2
RAINFALL mm	48	40	47	52	49	56	54	52	52	64	55	57
Days of Rainfall	11	10	11	12	14	14	15	15	15	16	14	13

6
Alice Springs, Darwin and the Northern Territory

The most enduring images left with the traveller to the Northern Territory are the flatness of its terrain and the incredibly vast, underpopulated isolation of the whole region. It is hard for visitors to grasp that one can drive for hundreds of kilometres without seeing another human being.

Given the inhospitable nature of the terrain it is hardly surprising that the Territory has a population of 168,600 (1991) spread over an area of 1,346,200km^2 (520,000 sq miles). Thus, while larger than every Australian state except Queensland and Western Australia, it has a total population only slightly larger than that of Geelong in Victoria.

The history of white settlement in the territory began in 1861–62, when John McDouall Stuart crossed the country from south to north. The subsequent route for the **Overland Telegraph Line** was devised using Stuart's maps, journals and other reference matter.

In turn, the repeater stations which were established along the Overland Telegraph route became the first communities in the Territory. The pastoralists soon compounded this by using the Telegraph Line as their chief stock route. To improve the water supply along the track, bores were sunk and, as a natural result of this activity, often where these bores were sunk a small community quickly developed.

The Northern Territory is still the '**outback**' and the people still have a pioneering spirit which has long departed from the urban south-east of the continent.

Don't Miss

*** **Uluru and Katatjuta:** spectacular rock formations at the heart of Australia.
** **The Devils Marbles:** unusual eroded boulders south of Tennant Creek.
*** **Kakadu:** a vast wilderness area of tropical savanna.
*** **Katherine Gorge:** dramatically beautiful.
*** **Litchfield Park:** waterfalls and swimming holes.
** **Arltunga:** a mining ghost town in the desert.
*** **Kings Canyon** and **MacDonnell Range:** spectacular gorges and scenery.

Opposite: *Darwin is a tropical city and its sunsets are a reminder of that intense climatic beauty.*

Climate

The Northern Territory's climate ranges from near-monsoonal at the Top End to typical desert continentality (hot days and very cold nights) around Alice Springs and Uluru. The Top End divides its seasons into 'wet' (Oct to Mar) and 'dry'. In the centre it is common for temperatures to fall below freezing at night-time.

Alice Springs

The second-largest town in the Northern Territory, Alice Springs has a population of over 25,000. Recognised as the '**Centre of Australia**' it owes its modern popularity to a booming tourist industry which brings people to '**The Alice**' to explore the beauty of **The Centre**, particularly the magnificent MacDonnell Range, or to head off to **Uluru** (Ayers Rock) and **Katatjuta** (The Olgas) which lie to the south-west.

Alice Springs is 576m (1900ft) above sea level and lies on the often dry Todd River. The springs, after which the town is named, lie to the north-east of the town and were discovered in 1871 by the team building the Overland Telegraph Line.

Prior to the arrival of Europeans, the area had been the home of the Aranda Aborigines who had been living in the area for at least 10,000 years.

The Repeater Station which was built at Alice Springs in 1871–72 was the first European building constructed in Central Australia. The station was closed in 1932 and is now open for inspection. Built of local stone, the station consisted of the postmaster's residence, an observatory and store room, the telegraph room and barracks. It lies 3kms (2 miles) to the north of the town. There are guided

Right: *The story of the early history of Central Australia would not be complete without mention of the Afghan camel drivers who helped to open up the wilderness. Today, the distant relatives of those early camels run wild or are bred at camel farms in the region. The farms offer interesting rides and longer safaris for those who are prepared to brave the back of a camel.*

tours each morning at 10:00. The town has a vast number of attractions for the visitor. A good starting point is **Anzac Hill,** which offers a 360° panoramic view of Alice Springs and its environs.

Adelaide House in Todd Mall was designed and built by John Flynn and was the first Alice Springs Hospital. The idea for a hospital was originally suggested by Sister Finlayson who arrived in the Centre in 1915 and was horrified to find that seriously ill patients had to be transferred by cart or wagon to Oodnadatta, which lies over 600km (373 miles) away.

On the corner of Todd and Parsons streets is the **Flynn Memorial Church**, built in honour of the late John Flynn who established the Flying Doctor Service. Today, the **Royal Flying Doctor Base** can be inspected at the southern end of Hartley Street.

In the **Old Pioneer Cemetery** there is a dramatic gravestone depicting a wizened old miner panning for gold. This is the last burial place for Harold Lasseter who believed he had found reefs which contained vast amounts of gold in Central Australia.

FLYNN OF THE INLAND

The Northern Territory has numerous memorials to the pioneering work of **John Flynn**, known as Flynn of the Inland. A Presbyterian minister, he spent 39 years of his life working among the people of the outback. He built nursing homes, established welfare centres and in 1928, founded the **Australian Inland Mission Aerial Medical Service** which used the pedal wireless to establish communication with outlying stations and properties. It eventually became the **Royal Flying Doctor service**. Flynn is remembered outside Alice Springs with a monument which includes a boulder from the Devils Marbles.

The locals have gone to some trouble to achieve fame through unusual tourist attractions. The famous **Henley-on-Todd Regatta**, held every August, is notable as a race along a dry river bed, and the **Bangtail Muster** in May is an occasion when numerous humorous floats parade down the main street.

AROUND ALICE SPRINGS

Simpsons Gap National Park is located just 8km (5 miles) west of Alice Springs on Larapinta Drive and is a 30,950ha (76,500 acre) park designed to preserve a piece of typical MacDonnell Range landscape. The waterholes, the ghost and red river gums, and the tame rock wallabies are particular attractions.

Henbury Meteorite Conservation Park lies 145km (90 miles) south of Alice Springs on the Stuart Highway. It is the site of a large number of meteorite craters. Scientists estimate that a meteorite crashed into the area about 7400 years ago.

Ewaninga Rock Carvings Reserve is 35km (22 miles) south of Alice Springs and contains some of the most interesting and impressive Aboriginal rock carvings in the Northern Territory. Unfortunately, their meanings have been lost over time.

Standley Chasm is one of the most popular tourist attractions around Alice Springs. Located 50km (31 miles) west of The Alice off Larapinta Drive it is a steep gorge within the MacDonnell Range. The walk into the chasm takes about 20 minutes.

Above: *The most popular of the many gorges in the MacDonnell Range is Standley Chasm, located 50km (31 miles) west of Alice Springs. The walk into the chasm takes about 20 minutes and, for those wishing to photograph the gorge in all its spectacular beauty, the best time is at noon when the sun strikes the walls on both sides of the chasm.*

Uluru and Katatjuta ★★★

In the language of the local Aborigines 'Uluru' is simply a place name which is applied to both the rock and to the waterhole on top of the rock.

There is some scientific disagreement about the origins of Uluru. The most widely held theory is that both Uluru and Katatjuta are remnants of a vast sedimentary bed which was laid down some 600 million years ago. The bed was tilted so that Uluru now protrudes at an angle of up to 85°. The rock is actually grey but is covered with a distinctive red iron-oxide coating.

In 1985, the title to the rock was handed back to the traditional custodians who, in turn, granted the Australian National Parks and Wildlife Service a 99-year lease on the park. Today, over 30 local Aborigines work in the park and the Board of Management is dominated by the traditional owners.

The caves around the base of the rock abound with hundreds of paintings which depict Aboriginal life. The caves to the left of the car park have quite a lot of interesting paintings and can be reached by an easy 10-minute walk around the base of the rock.

The decision to climb Uluru is one which should be based on fitness (it is only suitable for healthy people) and one's level of respect for the Aboriginal notion that this is a sacred site. The traditional custodians have resigned themselves to the inevitable despoliation of the rock, and climbing Uluru contributes to its despoliation.

The best time to see Uluru is at sunrise. At sunset, the more convenient time, there are literally hundreds of people jockeying for position in the sunset viewing area.

To the north lie the 36 smaller monoliths known collectively as Katatjuta (The Olgas). The highest is Mount Olga which rises to 546m (1790ft). The Olgas are spread across an area of some 3500ha (8648 acres) and the distance around the group is approximately 22km (14 miles). It is thought that Katatjuta may have once been one gigantic monolith many times the size of Uluru. Millions of years of erosion have reduced the single monolith to a series of smaller ones.

Uluru

Uluru (previously known as Ayers Rock) is a huge monolith – 862.5m (2850ft) above sea level and 1395km (865 miles) south of Darwin. It rises 348m (1142ft) above the surrounding countryside. It has an area of 3.33km² (1.29 sq miles) and a circumference of 9.4km (5.9 miles).

Left: *Uluru is one of the wonders of central Australia. The best time to see it is at sunrise when the light touches the vast rock and, slowly, its colour changes.*
Below: *The decision to climb Uluru is one which should be based on fitness and the visitor's level of respect for the Aboriginal notion that this is a sacred site. It is interesting to note that the average tourist stays at Uluru for 1.6 days and only 10% of all tourists actually climb the rock.*

Katatjuta is noted for its engravings and its geometric rock piles. Both the engravings and the geometric rock piles are believed to have been created by the Spirit Ancestor during the Dreamtime.

Kings Canyon ★★★

There is little doubt that Kings Canyon is one of the most beautiful sites in the whole of the centre. To be seen properly, however, visitors should plan to spend at least a day and, if fit and well prepared, do both the Canyon and the Creek walks.

The short Creek Walk is about 1.5km (one mile) and takes about an hour to return. It meanders up the centre of the canyon to a lookout point on the left-hand side of the valley, which affords a view of the sheer cliff face at the end of the canyon.

The Canyon Walk is a magnificent trek through the domes on the top of the canyon, with excellent views down the canyon from the walls at the top. The National Park rangers have estimated that this walk will take around four hours (and that's at a leisurely but sensible pace). The central attraction of this walk is the 'Lost City' a magnificent series of weathered buttresses of rock which look like the long-lost ruins of an ancient city or a moonscape.

There is also a valley known as the 'Garden of Eden' which has clumps of palm trees growing around a quiet and beautiful waterhole.

The Top End

Darwin ★★

The climate of warm days in winter and the long hot wet from late October to March, is monsoonal and the vegetation is typical tropical savannah woodland.

The area's prosperity has relied on Darwin's importance as a port, the cattle industry, and the mineral wealth which over the years has changed from gold to uranium. Today, it is increasingly geared to tourism, ranging from visiting places of natural beauty like Kakadu National Park and Litchfield Park to inspecting the museums, historic buildings and settlements which are reminders of the Top End's past.

Kakadu National Park Birds and Wildlife

As you enter the park on the Arnhem Highway the first place you will come to is the **Mamakala Observation Point**, a shaded platform from where the visitor can observe the edge of a wetlands lake with its rich variety of birdlife. **The Yellow Waters Billabong** is one of the most famous wildlife areas within the park. The accommodation at the Cooinda Motel gives access to the walks along the river, and the regular boat trips provide an opportunity to see birds, feral buffalos and crocodiles in their native habitat.

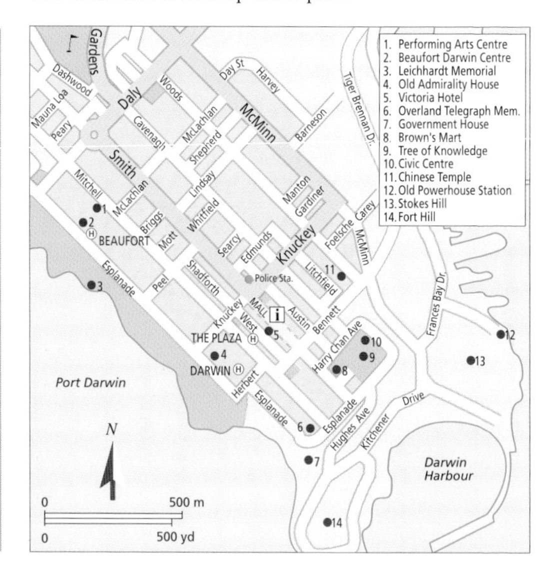

Darwin is a typical tropical township with a shopping mall and a few historical buildings that survived the three cyclones which have devastated the city.

To the south of Darwin there are a number of tourist attractions. On the Stuart Highway is **Crocodile World** where people can watch crocodiles being fed; on the road to Kakadu there is **Reptile World** with its hundreds of species of snakes and lizards; and then there are the boat trips down the muddy waters of the Alligator and Adelaide rivers to see saltwater crocodiles sun-basking in the mud.

The natural highlights of the Top End include the waterfalls (particularly Wangi Falls and the Florence Falls in Litchfield Park) which tumble across the escarpments, the fascinating magnetic anthills, the billabongs and vast wetlands with their myriad bird life, and the beautiful tropical sunsets and thunderstorms.

Opposite: *Darwin's popular East Point Reserve lies at the northern end of Fannie Bay. It is an ideal vantage point for visitors to look back across the bay towards the city.*

Below: *In 1872, Darwin's Government House, a seven-gabled house which overlooks Darwin Harbour, was built. It was rebuilt in the 1880s and is now known as the 'House of Seven Gables'. The house with its magnificent tropical garden is surrounded by a white fence.*

Kakadu National Park ***

One of the highlights of the Top End is Kakadu National Park. Listed by the World Heritage, it is now one of the most important wilderness regions in Australia covering an area of 1,307,300ha (3,230,000 acres).

Bounded to the north by Van Diemen Gulf, and to the east and west by the Wild Man and East Alligator rivers, Kakadu gained international publicity when it featured prominently in the two *Crocodile Dundee* movies.

Aboriginal Art in Kakadu

*** **Ubirr** is an Aboriginal rock art site of international status. There are ranger talks at Ubirr Rock Main Gallery at 09:30, 12:00 and 16:00; at the Namarrkan Sisters at 10:30 and 17:30; and the Rainbow Serpent at 11:30 and 16:00. Ubirr is one of the best displays of Aboriginal rock paintings open to the public anywhere in the Northern Territory.

*** At **Nourlangie Rock**, located south of Jabiru, there are over 100 sacred sites, some of them are designated sacred–dangerous (and therefore not open to the public). The area has a number of cave sites and there is evidence of quarries where the local Aborigines made their stone implements.

Mataranka and the 'Never-Never'

423km (263 miles) south of Darwin and 107km (66 miles) south of Katherine is Mataranka, a small, 4ha (10 acre) park with a superb thermal pool and stands of cabbage tree palms and paperbarks. Owned and operated as the Mataranka Homestead Tourist Resort, this is a popular stopover and picnic spot for visitors to the region.

The resort is near the site of Elsey Station, the subject of Jeannie Gunn's enormously popular autobiographical novel *We of the Never-Never*.

The park contains over 1000 plant species, a quarter of all the freshwater fish species found in Australia, and over one-third of all the bird species. Add to this the thousands of insects and the park is a reminder that the tropics are the breeding ground for the whole planet.

Katherine and the Never Never ★★★

If there is a region of the Northern Territory which is close to climatic perfection it would have to be the fertile and beautiful area around Katherine.

Positioned far enough south to avoid the worst excesses of 'the wet', and far enough north to avoid the harshness of the centre's desert continentality, the Katherine area has extensive beef cattle holdings, mineral wealth which exists from Pine Creek north to Kakadu National Park, and a burgeoning tourist industry.

The region stretches from the drier areas of Victoria Downs and Timber Creek to the mangrove swamps of the Gulf coast near Roper Bar. This area is flat, with the exception of the gorges in the Katherine region and the hilly country around Pine Creek, and covered with vegetation from tropical savannah to tropical woodland.

It has vast cattle stations which can often be up to 810,000ha (2 million acres) with herds of 40–50,000 head. At one time Victoria Downs Station was the largest cattle station in the world.

With the beauty of the Katherine Gorge, the large number of excellent swimming holes, the limestone formations which have produced Cutta Cutta Caves, the hot springs at Mataranka and Douglas Hot Springs, and the rich

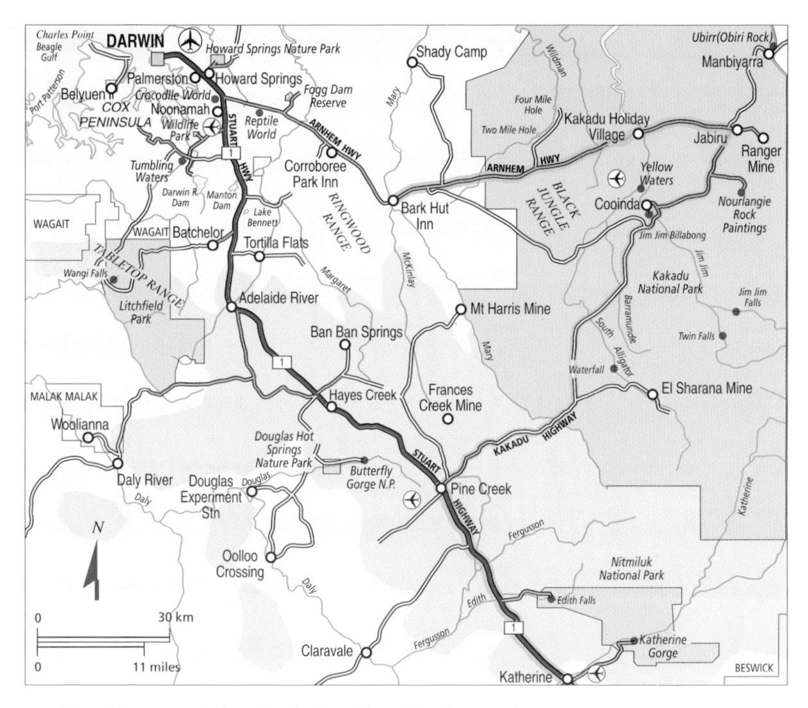

variety of fauna and flora (including the ubiquitous ant hills), the area offers visitors a range of delights.

The Barkly Tablelands ★★

Covering some 130,000km² (50,000 sq miles), the Barkly Tablelands area spreads from north-western Queensland into the Northern Territory.

This is a flat cattle-raising area with few attractions and consequently little to interest the traveller.

The distances through the Barkly Tablelands are vast and very monotonous. There are only three places of real interest – **Tennant Creek**, the mining settlement with its unusual buildings and interesting history; the **Daly Waters Pub** which is a genuine piece of outback history; and the **Newcastle Waters Station,** which offers a fascinating insight into the life of the drovers and the hardships of living in the Territory in the 1920s and 1930s.

Opposite: *Kakadu National Park, apart from a few small areas, is flat tropical savannah woodland with low-lying rocky outcrops. It is not, as many people think, tropical rainforest. It has been World Heritage listed because of its importance as a wetlands area, not because of its tropical splendour. Near this rocky outcrop are some of the most dramatic examples of Aboriginal rock art to be seen in Australia.*

Alice Springs, Darwin and the Northern Territory at a Glance

Best Times To Visit

The Northern Territory thinks in terms of dry and wet. **April** to **September** is the dry season. The climate is temperate and roads are accessible. During the monsoonal 'wet' (which starts in late October and continues through to March) all the dirt roads are closed. The only way to see Kakadu's spectacular **Jim Jim Falls** in the wet is by helicopter or aeroplane.

The weather around the centre is classic desert continentality. Thus, around **Uluru** and **Alice Springs** it is quite common to get temperatures rising to 40°C (104°F) during the day and dropping below 0°C (32°F) at night. Equally, the small rainfall produces a dryness which means that if you intend walking you need to take water to prevent dehydration.

Getting There

Darwin's **international airport** is 6km (4 miles) from the city centre. The **airport shuttle bus** will pick up or drop off almost anywhere in the city; book a day ahead when leaving Darwin, tel: (08) 8941-1656. **Taxis** are available and the major car rental firms have desks at the airport.

The major bus companies, **Bus Australia** and **Greyhound/Pioneer** run services from Darwin to Alice Springs, Tennant Creek and Mt Isa.

Alice Springs

Alice Springs new airport is 14km (8 miles) south of town. An airport **shuttle bus** meets all flights and takes passengers to city accommodation and railway. Major **car rental** firms have desks at the airport.

Darwin has an efficient local **bus service.** The city terminal is on Harry Chan Ave, tel: (08) 8953-2221.

The Tour Tub does a circuit of the city and stops at major places of interest. Darwin is well serviced by taxis and car rental firms.

Getting Around

Alice Springs

There is a limited public transport system for the town but Alice Springs is very compact and getting around on foot is easy.

Where to Stay

Darwin

All Season Atrium, cnr Peel St and The Esplanade, good-quality hotel with seafront position, tel: (08) 8941-0755, fax: 8981-9025.

Beaufort, The Esplanade, this luxury hotel is centrally located, known for its fine service, tel: (08) 8943-8888, fax: 8980-0888.

MGM Grand, Mindil Beach, luxury hotel and casino just out of the city centre, tel: (08) 8946-2666, fax: 8981-9186.

Budget Accommodation

Asti Motel, cnr Smith St and Packard Pl, quiet location, five-minute walk to city centre, reasonably priced, tel: (08) 8981-8200, fax: 8981-8038.

Darwin Travelodge, The Esplanade, quality hotel on the waterfront, reasonably priced, tel: (08) 8981-5388, fax: 8981-5701.

Alice Springs

Alice Springs Pacific Resort, Stott Ter, resort-type accommodation from family to deluxe categories, tel: (08) 8952-6699, fax 8953-0995.

Lasseters Hotel Casino, Barrett Dve, luxury hotel attached to the Alice Springs Casino facility, tel: (08) 8950-7777, fax: 8953-1680

Sheraton Alice Springs, Barrett Dve, luxury resort accommodation at the base of the MacDonnell Range, tel: (08) 8952-8000, fax: 8952-3822.

Budget Accommodation

Diplomat Hotel, cnr Gregory Ter and Hartley St, well-appointed motel, centrally located, tel: (08) 8952-8977, fax: 8953-0225.

Uluru (Ayers Rock)

This resort is managed by the **Uluru–Katatjuta National Park**.

Alice Springs, Darwin and the Northern Territory at a Glance

Sails in the Desert, luxury accommodation, tel: (08) 8956-2200, fax: 8956-2018.
Desert Gardens, comfortable, family-style living, tel: (08) 8956-2100, fax: 8956-2156.
Outback Pioneer, simple clean accommodation, tel: (08) 8956-2170, fax: 8956-2320.

Where to Eat

The NT Tourist Bureau puts out a free magazine which gives an up-to-date list of restaurants.
Cristos, Stokes Hill Wharf, excellent seafood restaurant in a delightful location, tel: (08) 8981-8658.
The Magic Wok, Cavanagh St, Wok cooking at its best, tel: (08) 8981-3332.
Rock Oyster, Mitchell St, Darwin's oldest and best known seafood restaurant, tel: (08) 8981-3472.
Siam, The Esplanade, Thai cooking, located in the Beaufort Hotel, tel: (08) 8941-2555.

Alice Springs
Bojangle's Bush Bistro, Todd St, cheerful restaurant with long bar and live entertainment, tel: (08) 8952-2873.
Overlanders Steakhouse, Hartley St, steakhouse with real outback atmosphere, tel: (08) 8952-2159.
Puccini's, Todd Mall, gourmet cooking, elegant surrounds make this an oasis, tel: (08) 8953-0935.
Miss Daisy's, Diplomat Hotel, excellent cuisine, tel: (08) 8952-8977.

Tours and Excursions

AAT King Coach Tours offers a comprehensive range of tours, 24-hour booking tel: (08) 8947-1207.
Breakwater Canoe Tours, offer a four-day canoe safari on the Daly River, tel: (08) 8984-4899.
Corroboree Cruise, cruise across the Darwin Harbour and watch an Aboriginal corroboree, enjoy a meal of barramundi under the stars, April to October, tel: (08) 8941-0744.
Top End Travel are Kakadu National Park specialists who provide action-packed safaris for the camper or those who want to be pampered, tel: (08) 8941-0070.

Alice Springs
AAT King Tours offer an extensive range of coach tours, tel: (08) 8947-1207.
Rod Steinert Tours offer a variety of outback tours, tel: (08) 8955-5000.
Aussie Balloons, view the centre from a balloon, tel: (08) 8953-0544.

Useful Contacts

Northern Territory Government Tourist Bureau, Smith St, useful publication, *Northern Territory Holiday Planner*, advice and bookings for tours available, tel: (08) 8981-6611.

Environmental Bio Diversity Group Parks Australia North, administers Kakadu and Uluru–Katatjuta national parks, tel: (08) 8938-1100, fax: 8938-1115.

ALICE SPRINGS	J	F	M	A	M	J	J	A	S	O	N	D
AVERAGE TEMP. °F	84	82	78	68	59	55	53	57	64	73	78	82
AVERAGE TEMP. °C	29	28	26	20	15	13	12	14	18	23	26	28
Hours of Sun Daily	10	10	10	9	8	8	9	10	10	10	10	10
RAINFALL in	1.4	1.6	1.5	0.5	0.7	0.5	0.6	0.4	0.3	0.8	1	1.4
RAINFALL mm	36	41	38	14	19	14	16	11	9	21	26	37
Days of Rainfall	5	5	3	2	3	3	3	2	2	5	5	5

7
Adelaide and South Australia

South Australia is Australia's third-largest state. It covers a total of 984,400km² (380,000 sq miles) of which just under half is nothing more than deserts of saltbush, mulga and seemingly endless sand dunes and flat, waterless lakes.

As a result, over 70% of the population live in Adelaide, and the rest are scattered in small settlements along the Murray River and around the coastline of Gulf St Vincent and Spencer Gulf.

The region which is deemed to be of the greatest economic value covers about 215,000km² (83,000 sq miles) in the south and south-east of the state. This is the area of the Flinders and Mount Lofty ranges, the Eyre, Yorke and Fleurieu peninsulas, and the Coorong and the Murray River valley.

Most of this area experiences cold, moist winters and dry hot summers. These conditions, which exist upon the coast, weaken further inland, eventually degenerating into areas of low rainfall and high temperatures.

History has been kind to South Australia. The two events – convict transportation and the gold rushes – which did so much to define the nature and character of most of Australia, are missing from the state's early historical accounts.

In 1829, Edward Gibbon Wakefield proposed a scheme for careful and systematic colonisation. A fleet of eight ships captained by John Hindmarsh left England and arrived at Holdfast Bay on 28 December 1836. The land near the site of modern-day Adelaide had been

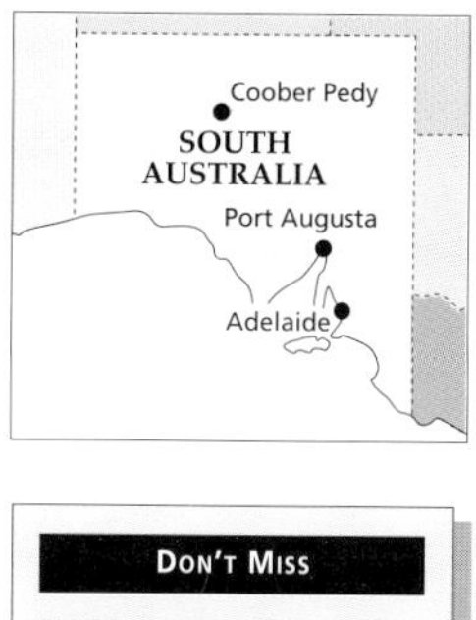

Don't Miss

***** Mount Gambier's Blue Lake:** a volcanic lake.
**** The Adelaide Hills:** towns nestling behind Adelaide.
**** Hahndorf:** a piece of Germany in Australia.
**** The Barossa Valley:** Australia's premier wine-producing area.
***** The Flinders Ranges:** dramatic desert scenery .
**** Port Lincoln:** where tuna fishermen reap rich harvests from the southern oceans.
***** Nullarbor cliffs:** dramatic cliffs on the edge of the Nullarbor Plain.

Opposite: *Adelaide's St Peters Church is one of the reasons the city is called 'City of Churches'.*

> **CLIMATE**
>
> Adelaide enjoys a typically Mediterranean climate with an average rainfall of 560mm (22in) and a temperature range from 12°C (54°F) in July to 23°C (73°F) in February. Most of the rain falls in the winter months and the summer can become very hot and dry.

surveyed and sold by March 1837, but surveys of country areas were delayed and property speculation became the colony's main industry. By 1840, only three years after first settlement, the colony had a population of 14,000 free settlers but was totally bankrupt.

Out of these unlikely origins, South Australia has managed to extricate itself so that now it is recognised as the centre of Australia's wine industry, a vital part of the nation's rich mineral base, an important area of secondary industry, and a state of great charm and beauty.

ADELAIDE

Spread out on either side of the Torrens River on the plain between Gulf St Vincent and the Mount Lofty Range lies Adelaide, an overgrown country town laid out in a series of easy-to-follow grids. Dubbed 'the city of churches' it is more the serenity of the city than the actual number of churches which inspires this notion of religious commitment.

Adelaide is a Mediterranean-style city designed for outdoor living. Its shopping malls, beautiful parks and the Torrens River flowing slowly through its centre are all conducive to leisurely walks and picnics.

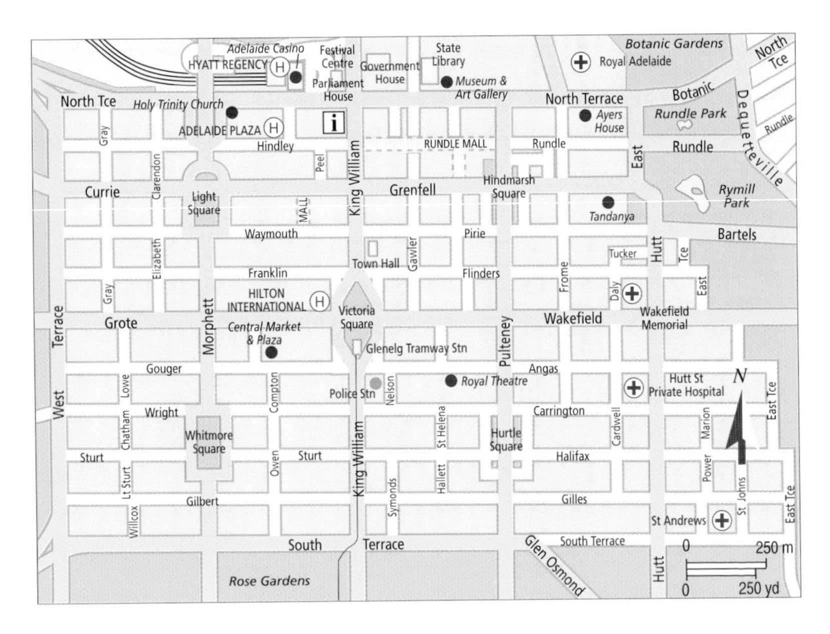

Left: *The Torrens River, the Festival Centre, the small modern city in the background and the boats for hire on the river banks are just some of the attractions that draw visitors to Adelaide.*

During the last half century Adelaide has sprawled. Its suburbs now spread for nearly 40km (25 miles) to the south, reaching almost to the McLaren Vale wine-growing area. To the east they nestle into the Adelaide Hills and, to the north, they spill into the industrialised sprawl of Elizabeth and Salisbury.

City Sightseeing

Any visit to Adelaide is really a three-pronged exercise. There are the historic buildings, the parks and malls, and the interesting outlying suburbs.

Art Gallery **

Located in North Terrace, the Art Gallery of South Australia is open from 10:00 to 17:00 daily. Admission is free. It is known for its wide range of early prints and drawings of colonial Australia. It also has excellent displays of South-East Asian ceramics.

Ayers House **

Situated at 288 North Terrace, Ayers House is an elegant Regency building which was built in 1846 for William Paxton. Today, the house, which has been restored by the South Australian Government, houses the National Trust of South Australia.

The Adelaide Hills

Once an area of small-scale farming, milling and cool summer retreats, the Adelaide Hills are now one of South Australia's most popular tourist destinations. At various times, it has supported mixed farming, sheep and cattle, vineyards, flour mills, commercial vegetable gardens and a rich diversity of arts and crafts. The small villages – Birdwood, Cudlee Creek, Blackwood, Clarendon, Glen Osmond, Gumeracha, Hahndorf, Lobethal, Mount Barker – are attractive and intimate.

Adelaide Zoo

Located on the banks of the Torrens River and surrounded by the city's superb Botanic Gardens, the zoo is over 100 years old. Inevitably this means that its 1500 exotic and native mammals, birds and reptiles are housed in a setting characterised by Victorian elegance. Its popular attractions include an Australian Wetlands Exhibit, a walk-through Australian Rainforest Exhibit and a re-creation of Seal Bay on Kangaroo Island. The zoo prides itself on its collection of endangered species which include the golden-lion tamarin, red panda, scimitar-horned oryx and Persian leopard. It is open from 09:30 to 17:00.

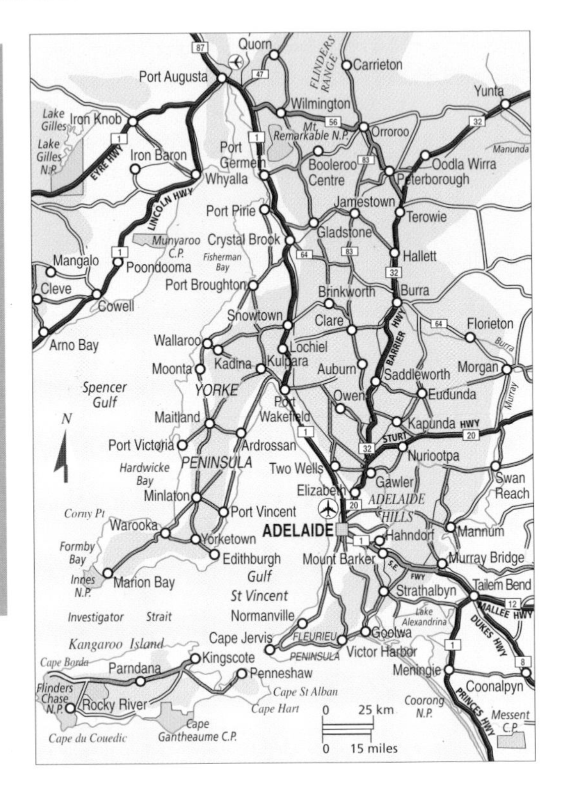

Botanic Gardens ***

This historic garden was established in 1855, and is one of the most delightful in Australia. Open from 07:00 until a variable closing time, it is a cool escape beside the Torrens River. Among the most impressive displays are the Museum of Economic Botany, a new glasshouse, a magnificent wisteria arbour and an avenue of Moreton Bay figs which were originally planted in 1866. Of equal interest is the State Herbarium, an institute for research which boasts a collection of more than half a million dried plants from all over the world.

Festival Centre **

An impressive arts complex on the banks of the Torrens River, the Festival Centre comprises a drama and lyric theatre, an open-air amphitheatre, an experimental theatre and a multipurpose concert hall. The venue for the biennial Adelaide Arts Festival, the complex offers a range of interesting cultural activities throughout the year.

Holy Trinity Church ⋆

Located at 87 North Terrace, this Anglican church is known as 'The pioneer church of South Australia'. The foundation stone was laid by Governor Hindmarsh in 1838. It was rebuilt and enlarged in 1844, and again in 1888. The church clock was made by Vulliamy, the clock-maker to King William IV and Queen Adelaide.

Tandanya ⋆

Home of the National Aboriginal Cultural Institute, Tandanya is located in the East End Precinct of the city. It provides a unique opportunity for visitors to experience living Aboriginal culture in its historic context.

Visitors will also want to explore the Rundle Mall and perhaps experience Hindley Street at night, Adelaide's answer to Sydney's Kings Cross. Further information can be obtained from the city's **Information Centre** on the corner of King William Street and North Terrace.

Suburban Adelaide

Glenelg ⋆⋆

No visit to Adelaide is complete without the 10km (6 mile) tram ride to Glenelg. Today it is a typical seaside resort. Historically, it was where Adelaide really started.

Of particular historic interest is the Old Gum Tree where, on 28 December 1836, Governor Hindmarsh reputedly read the proclamation declaring South Australia a British colony.

A replica of HMS *Buffalo*, the ship in which Governor Hindmarsh arrived, is located north of the centre of Glenelg. It is used as a restaurant.

The Adelaide Hills ⋆⋆

Once an area of small-scale farming, milling and cool summer retreats, the Adelaide Hills are now one of South Australia's most popular tourist destinations. Correctly known as the **Mount Lofty Range** the area, at various times, has supported mixed farming, sheep and cattle, vineyards, flour mills, commercial vegetable gardens and a rich diversity of arts and crafts.

Adelaide's Museums

Migration Museum: offers a rare and interesting overview of Australia's migration programmes since the early 19th century.
South Australian Museum: contains five floors of natural and cultural history with particular emphasis on the fossils, animals and minerals of South Australia.
Telecommunications Museum: a fascinating and unusual museum conveniently located in the city centre at 131 King William Street. It has separate sections devoted to different aspects of telecommunication technology.

Above: *Located 10km (6 miles) from Adelaide, Glenelg is a popular seaside resort where numerous holiday-makers admire the ornateness of the Town Hall, walk along the long jetty, play mini-golf in the huge Amusement Park, and watch the trams come and go along Jetty Road.*

Right: *While most of South Australia is desert, areas such as the rich grazing lands around the historic town of Penola in the state's south-east are ideal for the breeding of Hereford cattle.*
Below: *South Australia is famous for its grape growing and wine production. The Barossa Valley Wine Festival is held every two years and, apart from sampling the wines, one of the fun things to try is the ancient grape-crushing method.*

The streams which flow through the hills were ideal sources of power for the establishment of flour mills. At Birdwood, the famous Murray riverboat pioneer and adventurer, Captain William Randell, built a mill in 1852; at **Bridgewater** the old flour mill is now used in the production of sparkling wines; and between Hahndorf and Mount Barker stands another disused mill. Randell's mill is now home to the National Motor Museum.

Also found among the Adelaide Hills are a number of tourist attractions. There is a toy factory at **Gumeracha** which is home to the 'biggest rocking horse in the world' – an 18.3m (60ft) high 'toy. At Kersbrook there is a trout farm; Springfield has 'Carrick Hill', the former home of Sir Edward and Lady Hayward, on display; and Norton Summit boasts another vice-regal summer retreat.

The centrepiece of the whole area is, however, **Hahndorf** – the oldest surviving German settlement in Australia. The Germans, who settled in Hahndorf in 1840, were endlessly energetic and did much to establish milling, orchards and commercial vegetable growing in the area. Equally, they retained their cultural heritage so that today, Hahndorf still looks like a transported piece of Germany. It is the home of craftsmen, European-style bakeries, art galleries, and shops where German sausages and condiments can be purchased.

The Barossa Valley **

An important part of any visit to South Australia is a journey to the state's vineyards (located conveniently close to Adelaide) and an opportunity to taste some of the Barossa Valley's exceptional wines. The Australian wine industry established its reputation for quality in the valleys of South Australia.

Today nearly 60% of all grapes grown in Australia are harvested in South Australia. The state boasts no fewer than 150 wineries in towns and areas which are known both locally and overseas.

South Australians recognise 13 major wine areas, which produce wines ranging from cheap cask wines to gold medal, award-winning vintages. South Australian vineyards produce every kind of wine from reds to whites, champagnes, after-dinner sauternes, ports and sherries.

Undoubtedly, the most famous wine-growing area in South Australia is the **Barossa Valley** where, ever since the German immigrants arrived in the 1840s, wine has been grown commercially. The valley is small – 30km (18 miles) long and 8km (5 miles) wide – but within the area the soils, temperatures and rainfall vary so much that a wide variety of excellent wines are produced.

Over 100km (62 miles) to the north of the Barossa Valley, and nestled into the Mount Lofty Range, is the Clare Valley. Vineyards were introduced into this area in 1848, by the Austrian Jesuit priest, Father Aloysius Kranewitter. The area produces about 4% of the Australian grape crop and is home to such wineries as Stanley Leasingham, Quelltaler, Taylors and Fareham Estate.

Around the State

South Australia offers the visitor some of the country's most interesting scenery, ranging from the extraordinary desert which lies to the north of Port Augusta through the beautiful Flinders Range to the coastal beaches and the dramatic coastline around Port Lincoln and across to the spectacular cliffs at the edge of the Nullarbor.

Left: *The Flinders Range is spectacular. Wilpena Pound, the ghost gums beside the roads, the wilderness and the loneliness of the area, all help to make this an area which is uniquely beautiful and uniquely Australian.*

Right: *Nullarbor, from the Latin words 'nullus arbor', means 'no trees'. Today, the Nullarbor Plain refers to all the flatlands lying to the north of the Great Australian Bight. The Eyre Highway runs for hundreds of kilometres through countryside where there is nothing other than dry stunted grasses and low-lying hardy desert bushes. The effect is both monotonous and mesmerizing.*

The highlights include **Kangaroo Island**, at the entrance of Gulf St Vincent, which is the third-largest island off the Australian coast. It is recognised, particularly by nature lovers, as one of the best tourist attractions in South Australia. The absence of predators and any large, permanent human settlement has resulted in a rich variety of wildlife which feels totally unthreatened by the presence of people. Thus, at **Seal Bay**, visitors can walk among the seals. At the western end of the island the 60,000ha (148,000 acre) **Flinders Chase National Park** is home to thousands of species of flora and fauna.

To the east of Kangaroo Island is the **Coorong**, one of South Australia's premier national parks. In 1908, the poet Will Ogilvie wrote of it: 'It is sunset in the Coorong, the ribbon of blue water that divides the ninety mile desert from the sea…Great flocks of wild-fowl sweep and settle again with strange, discordant cries, and the white beach gleams.'

The northern and western half of South Australia is nothing more than desert. Sand dunes, searing summer temperatures, and scrubby inhospitable terrain have repelled even the most adventurous of explorers.

Kangaroo Island

Kangaroo Island, at the entrance of Gulf St Vincent, is the third-largest island off the Australian coast. It is 145km (90 miles) long and 55km (34 miles) at its widest point. **Reeves Point**, near the island's main town of Kingscote, is the site of South Australia's first Post Office and oldest cemetery. It is, by any measure, wild and beautiful. One early Australian writer's description of it was that, 'The southern coast of the island is bold, rock-bound and inaccessible, and long, heavy ocean-rollers break unceasingly upon it.'

The Flinders Range is the most extensive mountain range in the state. It stretches 500km (311 miles) from Crystal Brook, just south of Port Pirie to the southern edges of the Lake Eyre Basin. About 650 million years ago the range formed part of the sea bed. Its subsequent uplift has resulted in a series of fossils of sea creatures – trilobites and worms – appearing in the rock formations in the range. These are recognised as the oldest fauna fossils on earth.

The beauty of the ranges, and the establishment of the Flinders Range National Park (1972) and Gammon Ranges National Park (1970), has meant that tourism has become increasingly important. **Wilpena Pound** (a 'pound' is a synclinal basin) is an area of great beauty which has become popular with walkers and explorers.

The **Eyre Peninsula** was the first part of South Australia sighted by Europeans. In 1627 the Dutch explorer Peter Nuyts sighted the peninsula but, deciding not to land, turned back and headed towards Batavia.

The peninsula is sparsely populated and isolated, but the waters of both Spencer Gulf and the Southern Ocean yield a rich harvest of fish, southern rock lobsters, western king prawns, abalone, scallops and Coffin Bay oysters, which are all brought in to Port Lincoln.

At the northern end of the peninsula, **Whyalla** is the centre of the state's steel industry and is one of the most important steel-producing cities in Australia.

The Nullarbor Plain is an arid, scrubby, flat limestone plateau which, when it reaches the Southern Ocean, falls away dramatically in a series of sheer cliffs which tumble as far as 100m (330ft) into the cold seas.

The Nullarbor has the longest straight section of railway track in the world. It is virtually uninhabited. The region experiences less that 250mm (10in) of rainfall per annum, but because of the porous nature of the limestone the rain drains underground so quickly that streams cannot form.

In recent years, both archaeologists and speleologists have found elaborate cave systems under the plain's harsh exterior. The **Mullamullang cave** in the Madura district is now recognized as the largest cave in Australia. The **Koonalda cave** contains evidence of Aboriginal habitation dating back 18,000 years.

Left: *The cliffs of the Great Australian Bight lie between Nullarbor and Eucla. There are six clearly marked lookouts. A word of warning: none of the lookout points are for the faint-hearted or for people who can't stand heights. Here the cliffs rise sheer for about 100m (330ft) from the sea, which pounds on the rocks below. There are no safety rails.*

Adelaide and South Australia at a Glance

Best Times To Visit

September to **November** (spring): Adelaide is noted for the magnificent spring flower displays which grace the large parks and gardens throughout the city. From **March** to **May** (autumn) the cooler days and changing leaves turn the city's deciduous trees into a magnificent autumn display. During summer the city can become oppressively hot and dry. Many residents leave for the hills or the numerous beach resorts along the coast to the north and south of the city.

Getting There

Adelaide's **international airport** is 8km (5 miles) west of the city centre. **Transit Mini Buses** operate a service between the airport and most hotels, the city centre drop-off point is Victoria Square. Transit time is usually less than 35 minutes. **Taxis** are readily available and major **car rental** facilities are represented. Best to book ahead if you want a car to meet you.

Getting Around

Adelaide has an integrated **bus** service run by the State Transit Authority. The city centre has a **free bus** service and the **Bee Line Bus Service** operates around the city centre, running from King William St to Victoria Square. It operates every 5 minutes between 08:00 and 18:00. **The Glenelg tram** (a vintage 1929 model) travels regularly from the city centre to the beachside suburb of Glenelg. It is a delightful trip which provides the visitor with a short journey through suburban Adelaide.
Trains are available to the suburbs of Adelaide. For interstate travel the terminal is in **Keswick**, tel: (08) 8231-7699, for information and bookings. For the more adventurous the popular **Ghan railway** runs between Adelaide and Alice Springs. The journey usually takes 23 hours. **Taxi cabs** are readily available in the city, and all hotels and motels have extensive car rental listings.

Where to Stay

Adelaide has an extensive selection of accommodation, from five-star hotels in the city centre to popular bed and breakfasts in the suburbs.
Hilton International Adelaide, Victoria Sq, central location, luxury hotel, tel: (08) 8217-2000, fax: 8217-2001.
Hindley Parkroyal, Hindley St, well-located hotel with excellent facilities, tel: (08) 8231-5552, fax: 8237-3800.
Stamford Grand, Glenelg, best hotel in this beautiful beach suburb, short tram ride to city centre, tel: (08) 8376-1222, fax: 8376-1111.
Stamford Plaza, Adelaide North Ter, Adelaide's most elegant hotel, offers service and views to match, tel: (08) 8217-7552, fax: 8231-7572.

Budget Accommodation
Adelaide's Bed and Breakfast, Franklin St, simple living in historic sandstone building (1870), city centre, tel: (08) 8231-3124, fax: 8212-7974.
Festival Lodge Motel, North Ter, well appointed, reasonably priced and centrally located, tel: (08) 8212-7877, fax: 8211-8137.
Grosvenor, North Ter, family hotel with a variety of room styles and rates, tel: (08) 8231-2961, fax: 8231-0765.

Hahndorf
This German village nestled in the Adelaide hills retains its 19th-century charm. It is one of South Australia's premier tourist attractions. Gift shops, old-world buildings and eating houses are all within walking distance.
Hahndorf Inn Motor Lodge, Main St, conveniently located for easy exploration, tel: (08) 8388-1000, fax: 8388-1092.
Hochstens Hahndorf Motor Inn, Main St, well located, some serviced apartments available, tel: (08) 388-7921, fax: 8388-7282.
Hahndorf Old Mill, Main St, built in 1843, the old mill has been turned into a motel and conference centre, tel: (08) 8388-7888.

Adelaide and South Australia at a Glance

Where to Eat

Although Adelaide does not have the variety of restaurants that Perth, Sydney and Melbourne enjoy, it still offers some excellent cuisine. Travellers prepared to explore beyond the city limits to the **Barossa Valley**, **Clare Valley** and **Adelaide Hills** will find top class restaurants. In Adelaide, **Hindley Street** is known for its ethnic food while **Gouger Street** has more traditional fair. Check the free booklet, *This Week in Adelaide*, available at most hotels and motels, for up-to-date listings.

The Original Barbecue Inn, Hindley St, large selection of charcoal grilled meat and salads, tel: (08) 8231-3033.

Amadora Restaurant, Leigh St, historic building houses this excellent steakhouse, tel: (08) 8231-7611.

Fishcaf, Flinders St, value for money fish restaurant, tel: (08) 8232-3660.

Jolley Boathouse, Jolleys Lane, refurbished boathouse on the Torrens River, tel: (08) 8223-2891.

Paul's Seafood Restaurant, Gouger St, best fried fish in Australia, so it is said, tel: (08) 8231-9778.

Old Parliament House, North Terrace beside Old Parliament House, charming and intimate, tel: (08) 8211-8361.

Hahndorf

Hahndorf has built its culinary reputation on superb German cooking but the village has many other culinary delights.

Edelweiss Essenhaus, Main St, good German cooking, fun atmosphere, tel: (08) 8388-7366.

Hahndorf Hofbrauhaus, Main St, a taste of Germany, tel: (08) 8388-7888.

Hahndorf Cottage Steak House, Main St, something a little different in this German outpost, tel: (08) 8388-7454.

Tours and Excursions

South Australian Government Travel Centre, which is located at the Torrens River end of King William Street, conducts a variety of tours. One of the most popular is the Adelaide Heritage Walk, tel: (08) 8303-2033.

Adelaide Sightseeing Coach Tours offers a comprehensive tour of the city, tel: (08) 8231-4144.

Premier Tours offers trips to Hahndorf, Birdwood Mills and the Torrens Gorge, as well as other tours. These are well organised tours of the best attractions in the Adelaide Hills, tel: (08) 8233-2744.

E&K Mini-Tours offers the wine lover a Barossa day tour including lunch. The tour includes visits to a number of the more prominent wineries in this fascinating area, tel: (08) 8337-8739.

True Blue Tours have a three-day package to the Flinders Range. If you want a quick visit to the rugged desert beauty of Australia this is an effective way to experience one of South Australia's natural wonders, tel: (08) 8296-0938.

Useful Contacts

The South Australian Government Travel Centre, King William St, tel: (08) 8303-2033, Mon–Fri 09:00–17:00, Sat–Sun 09:00–14:00.

The Royal Automobile Association of South Australia, Hindmarsh Square has an excellent bookshop and provides helpful information and maps, tel: (08) 8223-4555.

Suburban Taxi Service, tel: (08) 8211-8888,

United Yellow Cabs, tel: (08) 8223-3111.

ADELAIDE	J	F	M	A	M	J	J	A	S	O	N	D
AVERAGE TEMP. °F	75	75	72	64	59	53	52	53	57	63	68	72
AVERAGE TEMP. °C	24	24	22	18	15	12	11	12	14	17	20	22
Hours of Sun Daily	10	9	8	6	5	4	4	5	6	7	9	9
SEA TEMP. °F	68	68	66	64	63	61	61	59	59	59	61	66
SEA TEMP. °C	20	20	19	18	17	16	16	15	15	15	16	19
RAINFALL in	0.8	0.8	1	1.7	2.7	2.8	2.6	2.4	2	1.7	1.2	1
RAINFALL mm	20	21	24	44	68	72	67	62	51	44	31	26
Days of Rainfall	4	4	5	9	13	15	16	16	13	11	8	6

8
Perth and Western Australia

Western Australia, the nation's largest state, is a vast, underpopulated, predominantly desert area like nowhere else in Australia.

It is basically a vast low-lying plateau which rarely rises above 600m (2000ft). The monotonous topography of the state is broken only by the narrow coastal plain which runs down the west coast from Broome to Albany, the low-lying Stirling Range in the south, and the Hamersley Range in the north-west.

Beyond the coastal plain the country degenerates into endless desert. In the centre of the state is the Gibson Desert. In the south the Great Victoria Desert and Nullarbor Plain sprawl across from South Australia. This vast desert wasteland means that, in spite of the state's area, most Western Australians cling to the coast. Less than 15% of the state's population live in rural areas and over 90% live in the fertile South West Land Division which encompasses both Perth and Fremantle.

Perth

Perth is known for its great charm and beauty. The elegant riverside parks, the network of freeways and the languid beauty of the Swan River all combine to give the city grace and distinction.

Kings Park ***

Otherwise known as Mount Eliza, Kings Park is the logical place to start city sightseeing. It offers a superb orientating view of Perth and the graceful Swan River.

Don't Miss

***** The Pinnacles:** strange shapes surrounded by sand dunes near Jurien, north of Perth.
**** Wave Rock:** near Hyden – an extraordinary wave-shaped rock.
**** Broome:** a tropical town with a fascinating past.
***** Kalbarri National Park:** the greatest wildflower display in Australia.
**** Kalgoorlie:** great gold-mining town.
***** Monkey Mia:** famous for the dolphins.

Opposite: *The Manning Gorge in the Kimberley offers cool relief in a dry and harsh landscape.*

Above: *Standing out among the solid Victorian buildings on St Georges Terrace is London Court, a narrow shopping alley notable for its mock Tudor frontages and its models of famous English characters.*

There are a number of interesting brochures on Kings Park. *Guide to Kings Park Botanic Garden* provides a brief history of the gardens and a map identifying the stands of jarrah, karri, tuart and heath in the park. The area has also been planted with flora taken from other 'Mediterranean' climates such as California and South Africa.

London Court ★★

Located on St Georges Terrace, Perth's financial and professional centre, this delightful alley with its mock Tudor frontage buildings is a popular meeting place for people shopping in the Hay Street Pedestrian Mall.

The attractive arcade features models of Dick Whittington, St George and the Dragon, Sir Walter Raleigh and imitations of Big Ben in London and the Grosse Horloge in Rouen.

Barracks Archway ★

Located at the top of St Georges Terrace, Barracks Archway is all that remains of the huge Pensioner's Barracks which once comprised 120 rooms. The arch is nothing more than a hint of the grandeur which once characterised this chequered building, completed in 1863 and used by the Pensioner Guards (retired soldiers) until 1904.

Central Government Precinct ★★

The original heart of Perth is a compact group of 19th-century buildings, close to the site where a tree was felled in 1829 to mark the foundation of the capital. The group of buildings occupies almost an entire city block.

The Central Government Building (1874–1902) has a plaque on its east corner from where all distances are measured. The Perth Town Hall (1867) was built by convict labour. The Deanery (1859) retains its shingle roof. Government House (1864) is surrounded by an English cottage garden.

CLIMATE

The state's climate ranges from tropical in the north, through arid desert in the west, to mild Mediterranean in the south. In the north, the monsoonal wet season sweeps across the Kimberley between December and March. The state's south-west corner enjoys a Mediterranean climate of cool wet winters and warm dry summers.

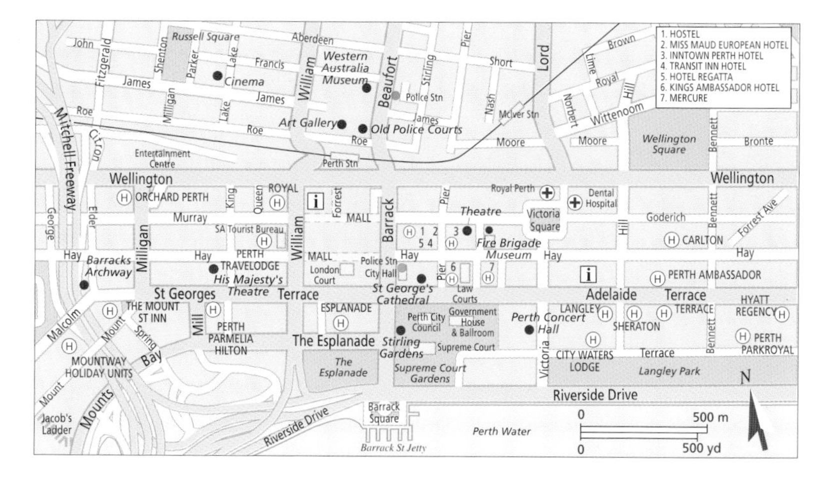

Cloisters ★★

Built in 1858 and located on St Georges Terrace just opposite Mill Street, the Cloisters have been a boys' school, a girls' school, private houses, a training college for clergymen, a university hostel and a café. The Cloisters are now part of the Mount Newman office block.

East Murray Street Precinct ★★

The East Murray Street Precinct, with its large Moreton Bay fig (listed on the National Estate) and its collection of harmonious buildings, is an ideal walk for anyone wanting to recall Perth's glories, when gold had made the state rich.

CITY OF PERTH

Things to do in Perth:

- Investigate the East Murray Street Precinct.
- Board a boat for a trip along the Swan River.
- Spend a day at Rottnest Island.
- Head for Fremantle and wander around its historic precincts.
- Stroll through the city's excellent parks and gardens.
- Explore Perth's many Heritage Trails.
- Try your luck at the Burswood resort casino.

Left: *Perth is the pulse of Western Australia. Its fortunes depend on the state's miners and graziers. In the 1980s, it buzzed with activity and its modern skyline reflects the rapid growth of that period.*

Above: *Rottnest Island provides the ideal 'car-free' getaway for busy Perth residents.*

St George's Cathedral ★★

Situated at the corner of St Georges Terrace and Cathedral Avenue, St George's Cathedral was designed by the eminent Australian architect, Edmund Blacket, and built between 1879 and 1888.

Stirling Gardens ★★

Located on the corner of St Georges Terrace and Barrack Street, Stirling Gardens are a wonder to behold in springtime. The blooms and the exquisitely maintained lawns offer a dramatic contrast to the canyons of iron and concrete surrounding the gardens.

St Mary's Cathedral ★★

Located in Victoria Square, this Gothic building was constructed between 1863 and 1865. Among the builders were the Benedictine Monks from Subiaco, who walked to the site every day to help with construction.

This is only a brief summary of the most prominent buildings in this historic city. For those sightseers wanting to investigate the history of Perth and its suburbs, a wide range of Heritage Trail brochures and booklets are available from the National Trust Bookshop in the Old Perth Boys' School building.

Eating Out

Visitors wanting a good guide to the city's restaurants should refer to *This Week in Perth and Fremantle* which is available free of charge in most hotels.

Beyond Perth

Western Australia's attractions are like those of no other state. The highlights are difficult to access (unless you travel everywhere by air) and involve vast distances. From the south to the north the state has extraordinarily beautiful beaches at **Esperance** (arguably the best in the

Rottnest Island

Located 19km (12 miles) off the coast from Perth, **Rottnest Island** is the city's favourite holiday and day tripping destination. Only 12 minutes by air and two hours by water, the island is an accessible location for those wishing to escape from Perth.

As recently as the last ice age Rottnest Island was connected to the mainland.

The **absence of cars** (everyone on the island rides a bicycle or walks), the historic buildings, the charm of the huge **Moreton Bay figs** and the quiet waters around the island, have been a magnet for Perth people since the 1850s.

There are a number of excellent Rottnest Island Heritage Trail walks.

country), a dramatic shoreline from Albany around to Bunbury, the great karri and jarrah forests of the south-west, the fascinating mining towns of **Kalgoorlie** and **Coolgardie**, the beautiful **Stirling Range National Park**, the historic **Margaret River** area, the coast to the north of Perth with the famous **Shark Bay** and **Monkey Mia** (where dolphins come to the shore), the strange mining towns of the **Pilbara**, the subtropical splendour of **Broome**, the dramatic **Bungle Bungles**, and the wild tropical outback of **Wyndham**, where crocodiles and the mudflats of five converging rivers make for one of the most unusual vistas on the whole continent.

The Great Southern Region

The Roaring Forties, blowing across the Indian Ocean, dump their rains on the southern tip of the state, producing a region known for its lush green forests covering its mountain ranges and spreading out into gently undulating valleys.

The area, which enjoys a Mediterranean climate, is also known for its vineyards. In the **Mount Barker** region there are a large number of small, specialist wineries producing high-quality Rhine Rieslings, Chardonnays, Cabernet Sauvignons, Pinot Noirs and Ports.

The centre of the region is **Albany**, a town of 20,000 people which becomes 40,000 in the tourist season. Lying 412km (256 miles) south of Perth, its superb deep-water, land-locked harbour was first discovered by Captain George Vancouver who sailed along the coast in 1791.

The forests around Albany are home to kookaburras, bush wallabies, kangaroos, emus and parrots. Ranging from forests to coastal wetlands, the region is home to over 3600 of Western Australia's wildflower species.

The beautiful, and appropriately famous, jarrah, karri and tingle trees were the basis for the area's timber industry. As early as 1884, the appropriately named Miller Brothers had established two timber mills at Denmark to the west of Albany. By 1905, most of the accessible timber had been removed and the area became a dairy farming region.

Vineyards at Margaret River

One of the great attractions of Margaret River are the **vineyards** and **wineries.** The climate in the area is perfect for grape growing. The first vines were planted as recently as 1967, but already the produce includes Rhine Riesling, Chardonnay, Semillon, Sauvignon Blanc, Cabernet Sauvignon, Pinot Noir and Shiraz. People wanting to do a little tasting should contact the Margaret River Tourist Bureau which has maps and details of opening times.
Contact (08) 9757 2147.

Esperance

The drive from Esperance west along **Twilight Beach Road** past **West Beach**, **Chapman's Point**, **Blue Haven Beach**, **Salmon Beach**, **Fourth Beach** and **Twilight Beach** is the most beautiful stretch of coastline anywhere in Australia.
The white sands, the gently rounded granite cliffs, and the ocean changing from aquamarine near the shore to a deep Prussian blue out near the islands of the Archipelago of the Recherche, is a combination of natural beauties which make Esperance one of the true wonders of the Australian coastline.

The sand dunes which have been pushed to fantastic heights by the unforgiving 'Esperance Doctor', are 50–60m (165–197ft) high.

Wildflowers at Kalbarri

Kalbarri National Park is one of the best National Parks in Australia. With nearly 200,000ha (495,000 acres) that become a vast carpet of wildflowers between August and October, the elaborate and spectacular twists and turns of the **Murchison River** as it cuts its way to the sea, the dramatic beauty of **Red Bluff**, and the equally dramatic beauty of the sandstone cliffs to the south of Kalbarri township, it's little wonder that this national park is rich in variety, drama and beauty.

The coastal waters of the region abound with fish, ranging from shark to salmon, flathead, whiting, silver bream, herring and groper.

The Midwest

The area known as 'the midwest' stretches from the ports of Geraldton, Kalbarri and Port Denison right across the state to the edges of civilisation on the perimeters of the Great Victoria Desert. In broad terms, the area divides into three regions – the Batavia Coast, the agricultural heartland, and the Murchison goldfields area.

The **Batavia coast** was first explored by Dutch sailors who were heading for the great trading port of Batavia in the Dutch East Indies. Crossing the Indian Ocean with the Roaring Forties, they were forced to head due north along the coast of Western Australia.

The economy of the area is primarily agricultural, although in recent times tourism – fuelled by the excellent climate and the variety of historical sites – has grown significantly.

Geraldton, with a population in excess of 20,000, is not only surrounded by sheep grazing, wheat farming and vegetable growing, but is also an important port for the export of grain, mineral sands and gold from the fields in the Murchison area.

To the north of Geraldton is the town of **Kalbarri,** noted for its lobster fishing. The town is on the edge of the Kalbarri National Park, a vast 186,000ha (460,000 acres) sandy park which has some of the best wildflower displays in the country. It is known for its emus, euros, rock wallabies, and red and western grey kangaroos.

Beyond the heartland lies the area of the Murchison goldfields, where the glories of the gold rush in the 1890s have now been overwhelmed by sheep grazing.

Below: *Located 586km (364 miles) north of Perth, Kalbarri National Park is noted for its wildflower displays and the spectacular gorges and rock formations cut by the Murchison River.*

Left: *One of the great tourist attractions of Australia can be found at Monkey Mia, where dolphins come to the shore to be fed by visitors. This is a rare opportunity for humans to make contact with these mysterious and wonderful sea creatures.*

Western Australia in the 1880s and 1890s was like Victoria in the 1850s. Men swarmed across the land in a desperate attempt to discover new goldfields. Paddy Hannan's discovery at Kalgoorlie, and the early discoveries at Coolgardie, had sparked true gold fever.

In 1891, the rush to the Murchison goldfields began when Tom Cue discovered gold at the town which now bears his name. In the years that followed, dozens of gold towns grew up only to die when the seams were exhausted and new ones were found elsewhere. Today, the area is a mixture of ghost towns and tiny settlements such as Cue (population 600), Yalgoo (423), Mount Magnet (1450) and Sandstone (380).

The Gascoyne

In recent years, **Monkey Mia** in the Gascoyne Region has received more attention than most out-of-the-way tourist resorts. This isolated beach at Shark Bay has created international interest because of the remarkable relationship which has developed between visitors and the local dolphin population.

For years it had been common for fishermen to throw the occasional fish to the dolphins. In 1964, a local woman hand-fed one of the dolphins. The dolphins returned the next day and so began a pattern of hand-feeding. Today, this unusual relationship between humans and dolphins has led to the establishment of the **Dolphin Information Centre**.

Cue – A Ghost Town

Known as the '**Queen of the Murchison**', Cue is located 650km (405 miles) north-east of Perth. At the turn of the century, Cue was the centre of the **Murchison Goldfields** boasting a population of around 10,000. Now all that is left is a small settlement (current population is around 300) with some of the most grandiose buildings to be seen anywhere in rural Western Australia.

Cue's buildings – most notably **The Gentleman's Club**, **The Old Gaol**, the **Government Buildings** and the **Masonic Lodge** – make a walk around the town a fascinating journey into the past. There are also interesting trips to unique **Aboriginal art sites**, the remnants of **Day Dawn** mine, and to the **Red Ochre** mine at Wilgie Mia.

> **Mining Towns in the Pilbara**
>
> The Pilbara is an area of mines, mining towns and port facilities. The exceptions – **Roebourne**, **Onslow** and **Cossack** – were the earliest towns in the region.
>
> In the last 30 years the four major mining companies – Hamersley Iron, Cliffs Robe River Iron Associates, Goldsworthy Mining Company and Woodside Petroleum – have invested over A$2 billion establishing major mines at Mount Tom Price, Paraburdoo, Shay Gap, Newman, Pannawonica, and Goldsworthy, constructing 10 new towns, building 1200km (745 miles) of private railways, developing and expanding five ports and completing two pelletising plants.

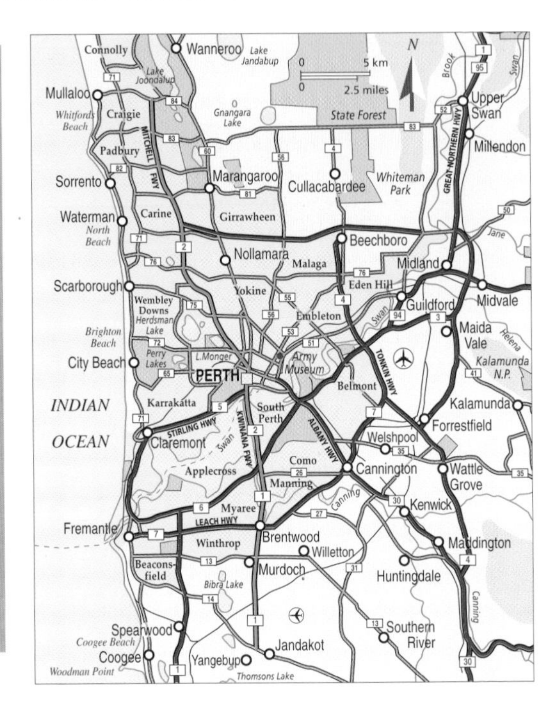

This fascinating tourist attraction happens to be in Shark Bay where both the first white man and later, the first Englishman, set foot on Australian soil.

On 25 October 1616, **Dirck Hartog** landed at Cape Inscription at the northern tip of Dirk Hartog Island, and in August 1699, **William Dampier**, the famous English adventurer and buccaneer, spent a week charting the shores of the bay. It was Dampier who named the inlet Shark Bay.

The Pilbara

Containing the largest iron-ore deposits in Australia, the Pilbara starts north of Exmouth, takes in the coastal towns of **Onslow**, **Karratha**, **Dampier**, **Roebourne**, **Cossack**, **Point Sampson**, **Wickham** and **Port Hedland** and runs east through the **Hamersley** and **Ophthalamia ranges** to the edges of the **Great Sandy** and **Gibson deserts**.

The coast experiences blisteringly hot summer weather and monsoonal rains which still produce only an annual average at Onslow of 334mm (13in).

Inland from the coast, nearly all the towns are, or were, company mining towns. The only exceptions (and only because they pre-dated the concept of the company mining town) are **Nullagine** and **Marble Bar**. Both towns grew in the 1890s as a direct result of the discovery of gold in the area.

Marble Bar, once a thriving gold-mining town, is now a tiny settlement of 350 people living in an area widely recognised as the hottest in Australia. The temperature from November to February is consistently over 40°C (104°F) and with only 334mm (13in) annual rainfall, the town experiences a virtual permanent drought.

There is the highly controversial **Wittenoom** where asbestos was once mined. **Newman**, with its 7000 people, was built by the Mount Newman Mining Company as a town for its employees. **Tom Price** was constructed by Hamersley Iron after vast iron-ore reserves were discovered at Mount Tom Price in 1962. **Paraburdoo** was the second of Hamersley Iron's mining towns and **Pannawonica** was built by Robe River Iron Associates.

The mining towns are tiny oases in a vast desert. Were it not for the wealth which lies below the surface it would be unlikely that anyone would want to settle permanently in this inhospitable region.

The Bungle Bungles

Known to the local Aborigines as **Purnululu**, the Bungle Bungles are located north-east of Halls Creek (take the Great Northern Highway 109km (68 miles) north from Halls Creek and turn east on the Spring Creek Track) on a road which is so bad that the RAC has this to say about it: 'The distance from the highway to the Three–Ways intersection is only 55km (35 miles), however, the trip will take two or three hours and the track is suitable only for 4WDs with good clearance. Caravans will not survive the trip.' Reaching the campsites involves further travelling for at least another hour.The journey is worth the effort as they are one of the natural wonders of Australia.

Left: *In 1887, the tramway at Cossack in the Pilbara area ran six horse-drawn passenger coaches.*

Above: *Dating back over 350 million years, the Bungle Bungles are formed from sandstone so fine that it crumbles when touched.*

The Kimberley

This vast area of north-west Western Australia is primarily cattle country. The monsoonal rains that sweep across the region from November to March produce a distinct 'dry' and 'green' season.

Three times the size of England, the Kimberley has over half of its area taken up by only 93 cattle leases. Not surprisingly, it is a region of considerable contrasts. Inland there is the spectacular and unusual beauty of the **Purnululu (Bungle Bungle) National Park**, while on the coast there is the multicultural melting pot of Broome.

The Kimberley is traversed by the Great Northern Highway which runs from Broome across to Darwin. **Broome**, with its small population of 5800, was once the pearling capital of the world (in 1910 there were over 350 luggers operating out of Broome). Today it is a combination of pearling, tourism, fishing, oil exploration and, in the hinterland, cattle grazing. The area is alive with dangerous animals, in particular, crocodiles. As the tourist brochure for the area explains:

- There is potential danger anywhere saltwater crocodiles occur. If there is any doubt, do not swim, canoe or use small boats in estuaries, tidal rivers, deep pools or mangrove shores.
- Be aware. Keep your eyes open for large crocodiles. Children and pets are at particular risk in the water or at the water's edge.
- Do not paddle, clean fish, prepare food or camp at the water's edge. Fill a bucket with water and do your chores at least five metres away. Returning regularly to the same spot at the water's edge is dangerous.
- Stand at least a few metres back from the water's edge when fishing. Crocodiles have not been known to attack well away from the water.

The Lord of Broome

There's an argument that says that Broome should be renamed McAlpine because Lord Alistair McAlpine so dominates the townscape and the economy of the town. Two of the town's most interesting buildings, **Matso's Store** and **Captain Gregory's House** were both restored and relocated by him.

McAlpine has converted this pearling port into a very attractive town. He has attracted government money to the town and has built a holiday resort at **Cable Beach** which is far removed from the day-to-day problems of the town.

Left: *Dawn over Broome Harbour captures the tropical splendour of this most isolated town. Once a thriving pearling port, Broome is today a tourist attraction for travellers wanting to experience something far removed from city living.*

Below: *To the north of Fitzroy Crossing in the Kimberley is the Giekie Gorge National Park. Famed for its cool, refreshing waters and its dramatic cliffs, this section also boasts a large population of freshwater crocodiles.*

Apart from crocodiles there are five varieties of pythons, brown snakes and death adders to be found in the region, and fishermen should be wary of stonefish, sea snakes and sharks.

Fitzroy Crossing, a traditional crossing point and resting place, is surrounded by cattle stations. **Halls Creek**, once a gold-mining town with a population of 10,000, is today another service centre for the outlying cattle stations. **Kununurra** was established in 1963 to service the Ord River Irrigation Scheme. While the scheme has been a limited success – 12,000ha (29,000 acres) are now producing peanuts, sunflower seeds, cucumbers, mangos, melons and pawpaws – the area's economy was enhanced when the Argyle Diamond Mine began production in the early 1980s.

The state's northernmost port is **Wyndham**. With a population of 1500 (which was significantly reduced in 1985, when the local meatworks closed down) it acts as a service town for the local cattle stations and various mineral exploration teams. It has become an ideal place for tourists to inspect crocodiles. There is a huge 30m (100ft) long crocodile replica in the town.

Perth and Western Australia at a Glance

Best Times To Visit

September to **November** (spring), to take advantage of the beautiful wildflower displays which Western Australia is justifiably famous for.

December to **February**, long, dry, hot summers make beach and water activities a joy on Western Australia's long coastline. The rainfall is so low that every day is almost guaranteed to be sunny. Perth has a warm temperate climate with a short, mild winter and long, dry summers.

Getting There

Perth **International Airport** is 20km (12 miles) north-east of Perth. The **domestic terminal** is 11km (6 miles) north-east of the city.

Bus and **taxi** services are available from both terminals. Transfer time is 30 to 40 minutes by bus, which stops at the **Airport Bus Service Centre** in the city and at some city hotels and motels.

Car rental facilities are also available at the airport. Advance reservations are recommended if you wish to have a car at the airport.

The famous **Indian–Pacific Railway** operates between Sydney and Perth and the **Trans–Australian rail** operates from Perth to Adelaide with connections to Melbourne. The Indian–Pacific is considered to be one of the greatest rail journeys in the world

Getting Around

Clipper buses operate five free city routes. The yellow route circles the city centre. It runs every 10 minutes, Weekdays 07:30 to 17:30, and Saturday 09:00 to 11:30. There are also red, green, yellow and blue routes which are clearly marked. **Transperth Buses** are the public bus company. They also link to the **ferry service** tickets which are valid for two hours and are used for both bus and ferry. **Trains** operate from Perth to Fremantle, Midland and Armidale.

Where to Stay

Perth has a large range of hotels and motels ranging from five-star luxury to numerous inexpensive hotels. **Mecure Hotel**, 10 Irwin St, quality hotel, with modern conveniences, tel: (08) 9325-0481, fax: 9221-3344. **Parkroyal Perth**, 54 Terrace Rd, luxury accommodation, overlooking the Swan River, tel: (08) 9325-3811, fax: 9221-1564. **Perth Parmelia Hilton**, Mill St, old-world elegance, in the centre of the city, tel: (08) 9322-3622, fax: 9481-0857. **Sheraton Perth**, 207 Adelaide Ter, comfortable and convenient, tel: (08) 9325-0501, fax: 9325-4032. **Sebel Hotel**, Pier St, excellent facilities well located, tel: (08) 9325-7655, fax: 9325-7383.

Budget Accommodation

Baileys Parkside Hotel, Bennett St, self-contained units, centrally located, tel: (08) 9325-3788, fax: 9221-1046. **Metro Inn Apartments**, Nile St, self-contained apartments and hotel rooms, close to city centre, tel: (08) 9325-1866. **Miss Maud European Hotel**, Murray St, Scandinavian-style in the city centre, tel: (08) 9325-3900. **Wentworth Plaza**, Murray St, comfortable and affordable accommodation, tel: (08) 9481-1000, fax: 9321-2443.

Fremantle

Historic Fremantle at the mouth of the Swan River is well worth a visit and is easily reached from Perth by train or bus. It has a mixture of beachside atmosphere with great historic interest. **Esplanade Hotel**, cnr Marine Ter & Essex St, international hotel in the heart of historic Fremantle, tel: (08) 9430-4000, fax: 9430-4539. **Trade Winds Hotel**, Canning Hwy, overlooking the Swan River, close to Fremantle, tel: (08) 9339-8188, fax: 9339-2266.

Perth and Western Australia at a Glance

Budget Accommodation

Old Bakery, Little Howard St, renovated bakery (1896), bed and breakfast style hotel, tel: (08) 9335-7531.

Where to Eat

Perth has an exceptional range of restaurants from traditional European cuisine to all types of Asian and Indian food. Check the free booklet, *This Week in Perth and Fremantle* for up-to-date listings. It is not comprehensive but it offers a good guide to some of the best eateries. It can usually be obtained from tourist offices and large city hotels.

Burbon Street Barron Eatery, cnr Hill & Hay sts, Mediterranean-style eatery, pasta and seafood a speciality, tel: (08) 9221-1339.

Darby's Seafood and Steak Restaurant, James St, cuisine for all the family, tel: (08) 9328-8744.

Golden Eagle Chinese, James St, traditional Chinese cuisine, tel: (08) 9293-2848.

Room With a View, The Esplanade, international cuisine, tel: (08) 9325-2000.

Trains, Planes and Automobiles, Lake St, Aussie-style in a fun and different atmosphere, tel: (08) 9328-2350.

Vino Vino, James St, popular Italian cooking served with style, tel: (08) 9328-5403.

Fremantle

Atrium Garden, Esplanade Hotel, excellent seafood at an affordable price, tel: (08) 9430-4000

Tours and Excursions

There is a range of excellent tours available from Perth, ranging from a short trip across to **Rottnest Island** to journeys to the wineries of **Margaret River**, a trip to **Monkey Mia** to see the dolphins, and journeys inland to the historic wheatbelt towns. Rottnest Island, daily ferry from Barrack St jetty. The trip takes two hours. An alternative is the Rottnest Airbus which will get you there in 15 minutes. Check with Western Australian Tourist Centre, tel: (08) 9483-1111.

Kookaburra Adventures, Beach Pony Express, tel: (08) 9228-1288. Half-day horseback adventure and beach ride, also going into **Yanchep National Park**.

Safari Treks, daily trips to the Pinnacles, tel: (08) 9271-1271.

Travel-About Outback Tours, trips to the **Pinnacles** or a four-day camping tour to **Kalbarri** and **Monkey Mia**, home of the dolphins, tel: 089 244 1200.

Captain Cook Cruises, tel: (08) 9325-3341 and **Boat Torque Cruises,** tel: 1300 368 686 provide scenic cruises of the **Swan River**, winery visits and trips to historic **Fremantle.**

Western Australia Tourist Centre has an extensive list of package tours from coach to paddle-steamers. Their information and booking service is free, tel: (08) 9483-1111.

Joy Flights, Royal Aero Club of WA, 30-minute flights over the city and beaches, tel: (08) 9332-7722.

Useful Contacts

Western Australian Tourist Centre, open weekdays 08:30 to 17:30, Saturday 09:00 to 13:00, tel: (08) 9483-1111.

The Royal Automobile Club of Western Australia, tel: (08) 9421-4444.

Terrace Rent-A-Car, Perth, tel: (08) 9479-4900, fax: (08) 9479-1537.

PERTH	J	F	M	A	M	J	J	A	S	O	N	D
AVERAGE TEMP. °F	77	79	75	70	63	57	55	57	59	64	68	72
AVERAGE TEMP. °C	25	26	24	21	17	14	13	14	15	18	20	22
Hours of Sun Daily	11	10	9	7	6	5	6	6	7	8	10	10
SEA TEMP. °F	70	72	70	70	70	68	66	63	63	66	66	68
SEA TEMP. °C	21	22	21	21	21	20	19	17	17	19	19	20
RAINFALL in	0.3	0.5	0.7	1.8	4.8	7.2	6.8	5.3	3.2	2.1	0.8	0.5
RAINFALL mm	9	12	19	46	123	182	173	135	80	54	22	14
Days of Rainfall	3	3	4	8	14	17	18	17	14	11	7	4

Travel Tips

Tourist Information

There is a vast fund of information about travelling in Australia available from a variety of sources.
The Australian Tourist Commission provides good material, free of charge, and is located in major cities abroad, such as London, Chicago, Los Angeles, New York, Toronto, Auckland, Hong Kong, Frankfurt, Tokyo and Singapore, as well as Sydney.
Each state and territory has a Tourism Board with its headquarters in the state capital, as well as regional and interstate offices. These will supply maps, brochures and other information on accommodation, transport, restaurants and tours. Usually open 09:00 to 17:00 on weekdays and on Saturday mornings. The capital city addresses are:

Queensland
The Queensland Government Travel Centre, cnr Adelaide and Edward sts, Brisbane, Qld 4000
tel: (07) 3874-2800.

New South Wales
The Travel Centre of NSW, 11–31 York St, Sydney, NSW 2000
tel: 132077.

Australian Capital Territory
The Canberra Tourist Bureau, Level 13 CBS Tower, cnr Bunda and Alcuna sts, Canberra City, ACT 2601
tel: (06) 205-6666.

Victoria – RACV Travel Centre, 360 Burke St, Melbourne, Vic. 3000
tel: (03) 9607-2233.

Tasmania – Tasmanian Travel Centre, 20 Davey St, Hobart, Tasmania 7000
tel: (03) 6230-8233.

South Australia – South Australian Travel Centre, 1 King William St, Adelaide, SA 5000
tel: (08) 8212-1505.

Western Australia
Western Australian Tourist Centre, Forrest Place, Perth, WA 6000
tel: (08) 9483-1111.

Northern Territory
Northern Territory Government Tourist Bureau, 38 Mitchell St, Darwin, NT 0800
tel: (08) 8981-6611.

Most cities and towns have at least one information centre with details of local sights and booking facilities for accommodation and local tours. Remember, however, that many have links with the services they advocate and may not be strictly impartial.
The visitor centres and offices of the National Parks and Wildlife Service provide useful material for areas under its jurisdiction, and the National Trust offers free walking tour guides from its offices or, often, from local tourist centres.
Other useful sources are the motoring organisations which provide excellent free maps for members of affiliated organisations. Their addresses are:

Queensland – RACQ, 300 St Pauls Terrace, Fortitude Valley, Qld 4006
tel: (07) 3261-2556.

New South Wales
NRMA, 151 Clarence St, Sydney, NSW 2000
tel: 132132.

Victoria – RACV,
360 Burke St,
Melbourne, Victoria 3000
tel: (03) 9642-5566.
Tasmania – RACT,
cnr Patrick and Murray Sts,
Hobart, Tasmania 7000
tel: (03) 6232-6300.
South Australia – RAA,
41 Hindmarsh Square,
Adelaide, SA 5000
tel: (08) 8202-4600.
Western Australia – RAC,
228 Adelaide Terrace,
Perth, WA 6000
tel: (08) 9421-4000.
Northern Territory
Association of the
Northern Territory,
79-81 Smith St,
Darwin, NT 0800
tel: (08) 8941-0611.
For information on various tours and tour operators, contact the outlets listed in this section.

Entry Documents

To enter Australia a valid passport is required and, unless you are a New Zealander, you will need a visa. This can be obtained in advance from an Australian consular office abroad or, if you are an American travelling by Qantas, you can obtain one from the airline's offices in Los Angeles or San Francisco. Short-stay visas are valid for up to three months and long-stay visas for up to six. The former are free while the latter carry a small charge, as do multiple-entry visas. Extensions requested from within Australia can be costly. The amount of time you plan to spend in the country is not entirely at your own discretion. Embassy officials might limit your time if they do not consider you a desirable visitor. A return ticket and 'sufficient funds' are also required, although there is no clear definition of what 'sufficient funds' might actually mean.

A Working Holiday Maker visa exists for 'young' people (usually meaning 18 to 26) from Ireland, the Netherlands, the UK, Canada and Japan. It is available from the country of origin, valid for up to one year and carries a charge. It permits casual rather than full-time employment, meaning that you are only supposed to work for three of the twelve months. Fruit-picking is one of the most common, short-term job prospects. Visa extensions can take a long time to obtain and may be surrounded by lengthy procedures so apply as early as possible. A$50 fee must be paid up-front which will not be refundable, regardless of the outcome.

Air Travel

Australia is a popular destination so be sure to book well in advance, particularly if you wish to travel at major holiday times or via popular routes. Prices vary greatly depending on whether you deal with an airline or agent, the route you choose, the time of year etc., so shop around. Remember that some flights may be cheap for a good reason, entailing several stops and a long, uncomfortable journey. Townsville, Cairns, Darwin and all state capitals with the exception of Hobart have direct air links with overseas destinations (Port Hedland has flights to and from Bali), which creates the possibility of arriving and departing from different Australian cities. Visitors should recognise that Sydney (Kingsford Smith) airport is the country's major air terminal and this can mean delays with landing and customs.

An airport bus service usually exists to transport you into the city and remember that you will need to keep A$20 aside for the departure tax.

Domestic air travel is strictly non-smoking. For those who prefer the idea of travelling by sea, **P&O**, **CTC**, **Royal Viking** and **Cunard** still offer ocean cruises to Australia, albeit at a price.

Road Travel

The vast distances of Australia, and the lack of public transport in places like Alice Springs, can make car rental attractive if you are tired of tours.

The airports, cities and towns of Australia offer the visitor a large number of car rental agencies, both local and international. This competition means a range of prices and plenty of temporary specials, so investigate the options.

The major companies – **Avis**, **Hertz** and **Budget** – dominate the airports. They differ little on typical round-the-city rentals, but special offers emerge with less typical and longer-term deals. While unlimited kilometre rates are normal around the city, country and remote driving can incur a higher flat rate plus a kilometre charge. And don't forget insurance cover. Smaller companies are often cheaper, but certainly not always, even if they appear so at first. Be sure to read the fine print and weigh-up the pros and cons. A valid driving licence is, of course, essential when hiring a car and applicants usually must be over 21. One-way rentals between major cities are available but are not very economical. Note that smaller cars may be cheaper but are not as comfortable on a long journey. Restrictions may also apply with regard to crossing state boundaries and, depending on the type of car you rent, concerning driving on unsealed roads. A four-wheel-drive could be a wise choice for outback driving or a campervan for long distances.

Clothes: What to Pack

Australia enjoys long hot summers and generally mild winters. People dress informally, though 'smart casual' wear is often required after dark at theatres and other art/entertainment venues, and by the more sophisticated hotels and restaurants. Beach wear is acceptable only on the beach and in beach fast food and casual eateries; casual clothing is customary in most places.
For summer months (October to April), pack lightweight garments, a hat, and plenty of sunscreen. For travellers with very fair skin, a sun protection factor (SPF) of 15+ is the minimum. Remember, Australia has the highest rate of skin cancer in the world, and suffering from sunstroke, painful or peeling skin is a high price to pay for a 'golden' tan.
It can get cool at night. Most of the east coast experiences summer rains. Bring an umbrella. In winter, only Melbourne and Canberra get really cold.

Money Matters

Bank hours are usually 09:30 to 16:30, Monday to Thursday with an extension until 17:00 on Fridays, although, in some major cities, hours can be 08:00 to 18:00 Monday to Friday. Building societies are often open longer than banks.
Traveller's cheques are most readily dealt with, particularly if made out in Australian dollars, and typically receive a better exchange rate than foreign currency. However, virtually all banks will readily and efficiently change both, albeit with varying charges. A passport is usually sufficient proof of identity.
Credit cards are widely in use and preferred by car rental agencies but may not be so welcome in remote areas or smaller shops.
In Australia, there are 100 cents to the dollar. Coins come in 5c, 10c, 20c, 50c, A$1 and A$2 denominations and there are A$5, A$10, A$20, A$50 and A$100 notes. Any quantity of money can be taken in and out of the country, although, for amounts over A$5000 you must complete a form.
If staying for any duration you could open a cashcard account with a major bank, allowing you access to automatic teller machines (ATMs), which are very widespread and open 24 hours. The cashcards permit you to withdraw A$400 to A$500 a day and can be used to make calls in special phone booths distributed throughout the country. They are also linked to the 'EFTPOS' system (Electronic Funds Transfer at the Point of Sale) which allows you to pay for goods and services in some stores.

Tipping

Tipping is not standard practice in Australia. You may wish to add an extra 10% to the bill at a restaurant if you are impressed with the service, but it is not mandatory. Restaurant prices carry no extra taxes or service charges and the food in Australia is plentiful, high quality and cheap, although manufactured goods tend to be more expensive.

Waiting staff are paid the standard Australian minimum wage, so they are not dependent on tips, unlike their counterparts in other countries.

Trading Hours

These are from 08:30 or 09:00 until 17:00 or 17:30, Monday to Friday and 09:00 to 13:00 on Saturday, with late-night shopping on Thursday and/or Friday, when the shops close at 20:00 or 21:00. However, these hours vary somewhat in different centres. Major retailers stay open until 16:00 on a Saturday and most are open on Sundays. Major supermarket chains now tend to open seven days a week in more densely populated areas. Corner shops, milk bars, delis (the common term for a delicatessen) and city bookshops also open for extended trading.

Accommodation

There is a truly comprehensive guide to accommodation in Australia which covers all levels of hotels, motels, guest houses and rented accommodation. It is a joint production of the RACV (the Victorian road association) and the RAASA (the South Australian road association).
Titled *A–Z Australian Accommodation Guide,* it is published regularly and can be purchased from any state road association outlet. It is very detailed, providing star ratings as well as up-to-date information about prices and facilities. Anyone intending to stay in Australia for an extended period should purchase this excellent publication. No commercial publications can compete with it.

Electricity Supply

The electrical current in Australia is 220-240 volts AC. The local plug-and-socket system uses three pins. These are not the same as those utilised in the UK and only upmarket hotels and motels tend to have appropriate converters. Decent hardware stores may carry adaptors but, failing this, an Australian plug can usually be fitted to an electrical applicance from abroad.

Health and Personal Safety

Australia is a country with high standards of hygiene and very safe food and drinking water. As a result, special precautions are not necessary. No vaccinations are required unless some time has been spent in an infected country in the previous two weeks, although immunisation is always a good idea if your international itinerary is broad.
The intense sun, however, could be a problem, particularly for visitors from more temperate climates. Australia has a high skin cancer rate so be sure, if spending any length of time in its glare, to apply sun cream, wear a broad-brimmed hat, and a shirt with a collar and preferably long sleeves.
Australia offers free service at public hospitals to its own citizens and permanent residents, and has universal health care under the Medicare system. This covers either most or all of the cost of visiting a general practitioner, depending largely on whether bulk-billing practices are utilised. However, these services only extend to citizens of the United Kingdom and New Zealand. All visitors will have to pay in full and up-front for dental treatment, ambulance charges and medicines. The cost of an unsubsidised, standard visit to a doctor is currently around A$35 but remember that serious problems can become expensive. Travel insurance covering medical care and medicines is therefore recommended. A personal basic medical kit would also be a good idea. The telephone number for emergencies is 000, and both crisis hotlines and interpreter services are at the front of the White Pages of the telephone directory. Note that condoms are available at chemists, some all-night stores and at vending machines in the toilets of universities and some hotels. The pill is only available on prescription and so requires a visit to a doctor.

Health Hazards

When bushwalking be sure to wear boots, thick long

socks and long trousers, and be careful where you put your hands. Ticks and leeches are common in the scrub so check your body thoroughly after bushwalking as ticks can be dangerous if unnoticed. Ticks can be removed with kerosene or methylated spirits (don't break the head off inside your body) and leeches with salt or heat.
The chances of being attacked, stung or bitten by venomous wildlife are extremely remote but, if a poisonous snake or spider should bite, try to catch the offending creature as antivenenes are available, but don't risk another bite in the process. Stay calm, wrap the area in a tight bandage, as you would with a sprained ankle (DON'T use a tourniquet or suck out the poison), attach a splint to the limb, keep very still and send for medical help.
A similar procedure applies to poisons incurred from marine life. Sea wasps are a deadly type of jellyfish which sting with their tentacles, causing telltale welt marks. Douse the wound with vinegar and don't remove the stingers. Always wear hard-soled boots if walking on a reef because of sharp corals and poisonous cone shells and stonefish.
If travelling in the outback drive very carefully. Some roads are not well developed and the behaviour of other drivers is always of concern. If a huge truck (a road train) comes along, get out of the way as they most certainly won't make way for you.
Respect fire bans (broadcast on the radio) and be careful with cigarette butts and broken glass which can ignite bushfires in hot, dry weather. If caught in a fire, head for a clearing (avoid dense tree growth). Get off the road, stay in the vehicle, get under the dashboard and cover yourself, preferably with a woollen blanket.
If bushwalking or camping be sure to leave an itinerary with friends and go carefully prepared. Remember that nights can turn out to be freezing despite the daytime temperature.

Emergency

The national number for all emergencies is 000. This will get you connected to police, ambulance or other emergency services. All telephone directories have extensive listings of emergency services and facilities in the front section of the book.

Conversion Chart

From	To	Multiply By
Centimetres	inches	0.394
Inches	centimetres	2.54
Metres	feet	3.28
Feet	metres	0.305
Metres	yards	1.09
Yards	metres	0.914
Kilometres	miles	0.621
Miles	kilometres	1.61
Grams	ounces	0.035
Ounces	grams	28.3
Kilograms	pounds	2.20
Pounds	kilograms	0.454
Tonnes	tons	0.984
Tons	tonnes	1.02
Hectares	acres	2.47
Acres	hectares	0.405
Square kilometres	square miles	0.386
Square miles	square kilometres	2.59
Millilitres	fluid ounces	0.0352
Fluid ounces	millilitres	28.4
Litres	pints	1.76
Pints	litres	0.568
Kilometres	miles	0.621
Miles	kilometres	1.61

To convert Celsius to Fahrenheit: 1.8 x degrees Celsius + 32
To convert Fahrenheit to Celsius: 0.5555 x degrees Fahrenheit – 32

INDEX

Page numbers in **bold** refer to photographs.